# THE

# QUARTERLY

EDITED BY

GORDON LISH

Dear Editor Of The Mag;

    I am an Old Man of 88 years with not alott of time to kid aro und
with you, seeing as how I could Dro p Dead from anything any minute,
even from if somebody shouts to loud in my Direction. You probibly know
Me as the boyfreind of Mrs. Crackel,  your faithfull corispondent.
Anyway the reason I am writnig to Y o u is to tell you that I do not
now why Mrs. Crackel (retired) should shoulf reprisent The County Home
in your mag. She do   not know shit.Beleive me, as her Ex-boyfreind, I
can tell you. That Old Dame is so seemile seenile she calls me Sam in
her lettres, wh ereas my real name is "Nose Man." I would be honored to
be your new corisp ondint from here.Watch it you do no t say no to me.
Else I will send my new n ewn  new Girlfreind Marge (Pitzer,no t retired
79) to co me there to piss on yo ur fucking doo rstep for you.

                Y o urs In His Precious Blood,

                H o se Man Wo olley (Active)

WHAT ARE WE TO DO?
HOW ARE WE TO MAKE CLEAR TO YOU THE KIND OF MAGAZINE
WE ARE—OR ANYWAY HOPE TO BE? WITNESS: IT IS THE SEASON
OF THE YEAR WHEN THE TELEPHONE CALLS START PILING UP
WITH CALLERS PUTTING TO US THE SAME DAMN SILLY DAMN
GODDAMN QUESTION, THE WHICH IS, "HEY, YOU PEOPLE READING
OVER THE SUMMER?" OKAY, LOOK, LET'S STAY CALM, LET'S JUST
EVERYBODY TRY TO STAY CALM. ANSWER: YES, YES, YES, YES,
WE PEOPLE ARE READING OVER THE SUMMER. WE PEOPLE ARE,
FOR THAT MATTER, ALSO READING OVER THE NIGHT, OVER
THE MORNING, OVER THE WEEKEND, OVER THE HOLIDAY, OVER
THE VACATION, OVER THE DEAD BODIES OF ANYBODY WE HAVE
TO READ OVER FOR US TO KEEP UP WITH THE TASK OF WHAT
WE PUT IT TO YOU IS THE BUSINESS OF THIS MAGAZINE—TO WIT,
TO KEEP READING EVERYTHING IN SIGHT IN ORDER THAT WE
MIGHT KEEP CONVINCING OURSELVES THAT WE ARE READING
WRITING NO OTHER MAGAZINE WOULD HAVE THE STEADFASTNESS
TO READ BECAUSE EVERY OTHER MAGAZINE IS TOO BUSY
NOT READING OVER THE SUMMER OR OVER THE NIGHT OR OVER
THE MORNING, OR . . . WELL, YOU GET THE POINT, DO YOU NOT?
IT GOES LIKE THIS—YOU COME UPON A STUPENDOUS DEPOSIT
OF HORSESHIT. OKAY, NOW, YES OR NO—MIGHTN'T IT BE LIKELY
THAT DOWN THERE INSIDE IT SOMEWHERE YOU COULD
MAYBE FIND FOR YOURSELF A PONY?

# THE QUARTERLY

21/SPRING 1992

**VINTAGE BOOKS**

A DIVISION OF RANDOM HOUSE, INC.

NEW YORK

*THE QUARTERLY* (ISSN: 0893-3103) IS EDITED BY GORDON LISH
AND IS PUBLISHED MARCH, JUNE, SEPTEMBER, AND DECEMBER AT
201 EAST 50TH STREET, NEW YORK, NY 10022. SUBSCRIPTION REQUESTS—
FOUR ISSUES AT $48 US, $60 CANADIAN, $54 US OVERSEAS—AND ADDRESS
CHANGES SHOULD BE SENT TO THE ATTENTION OF SUBSCRIPTION OFFICE,
28TH FLOOR. ORDERS RECEIVED BY JANUARY 31 START WITH MARCH NUMBER;
BY APRIL 30, JUNE NUMBER; BY JULY 31, SEPTEMBER NUMBER; BY OCTOBER 31,
DECEMBER NUMBER. SEE LAST PAGE FOR PURCHASE OF BACK NUMBERS.

MANAGEMENT BY ELLEN F. TORRON
COORDINATION BY GEORGE DONAHUE
DESIGN BY ANDREW ROBERTS
ART DIRECTION BY CATHRYN S. AISON AND REBECCA AIDLIN
EDITORIAL ASSISTANCE BY RICK WHITAKER AND COLIN DICKERMAN

*THE QUARTERLY* WELCOMES THE OPPORTUNITY TO READ WORK OF EVERY
CHARACTER, AND IS ESPECIALLY CONCERNED TO KEEP ITSELF AN OPEN FORUM.
MANUSCRIPTS MUST BE ACCOMPANIED BY THE CUSTOMARY RETURN MATERIALS,
AND SHOULD BE ADDRESSED TO THE EDITOR. *THE QUARTERLY* MAKES THE UTMOST
EFFORT TO OFFER ITS RESPONSE TO MANUSCRIPTS NO LATER THAN ONE WEEK
SUBSEQUENT TO RECEIPT. OPINIONS EXPRESSED HEREIN ARE NOT NECESSARILY
THOSE OF THE EDITOR OR OF THE PUBLISHER.

ISBN: 0-679-73862-2

THE HOB BROUN PRIZE FOR 1991 IS AWARDED TO DAWN RAFFEL, FOR "IN
THE YEAR OF LONG DIVISION," AND TO CHRISTINE SCHUTT, FOR
"YOU DRIVE," WHICH WORK APPEARED IN *Q*18 AND *Q*20. IN RESPECT OF
THESE MATTERS, *Q* READERS WILL JOIN THE EDITOR IN HIS SAD NOTE OF
THE PASSING OF JANE BROUN, MOTHER OF HOB BROUN, WIFE OF THE INESTIMABLY
BRAVE HEYWOOD HALE BROUN, WHOSE GIFT ENABLES THE CONTINUITY OF
THE LITERARY ACKNOWLEDGMENT ENACTED IN HIS DECEASED SON'S NAME. HEY, IS
THIS A GOOD THING OR A BAD THING? THE FACT THAT DANIEL QUINN, A FORMER
*Q*-ER (NO REASON WHY HE CANNOT BE A FUTURE *Q*-ER, TOO, ONE SUPPOSES) HAS
JUST DISCOVERED HIMSELF IN RECEIPT OF $500,000 (YOU HEARD US, PAL, WE
SAID FIVE HUNDRED THOUSAND DOLLARS) BY REASON OF HIS WRITERLY EXERTIONS,
THESE BEING SUMMED UP UNDER THE TITLE *ISHMAEL*, A NOVEL SO FAVORED BY
A PANEL OF READERS IN THE EMPLOY OF TED TURNER (THE CNN-ER, THAT IS)
THAT IT, THE PANEL, COULD DO NAUGHT BUT TURN OVER TO QUINN TURNER'S BIG
BUCKS. SO BACK TO THE QUESTION—IS THIS A GOOD THING OR IS THIS A BAD
THING? THE ANSWER IS IT'S A GOOD THING. AT LEAST FROM THE STANDPOINT
OF THE GNP. WELL, ALSO FROM THE STANDPOINT OF MRS. QUINN. EVEN FROM
THE STANDPOINT OF THE WHOLE TOWN OF AUSTIN, TEXAS, WHERE, WE GUESS,
THE QUINNS WILL BE SPENDING NO LITTLE OF THE TURNER LUCRE. ACTUALLY,
THERE'S ANOTHER STANDPOINT IT'S A GOOD THING FROM, WHICH IS THAT QUINN,
DANIEL QUINN—TAKE OUR WORD FOR IT—IS AN ABSOLUTE PEACH OF A FELLOW.

# THE QUARTERLY

21 / SPRING 1992

# THE QUARTERLY

CAN YOU BEAT IT? A TABLE OF CONTENTS THAT FAILS
TO RUN TO OUR ROUTINE LENGTH. OH MY, OH MY,
WHAT EVER IS THE MATTER? OR WAS. WELL, FINE, FINE,
HERE'S THE ANSWER FOR YOU—GREG MULCAHY'S NOVEL
*GLASS*. THAT'S RIGHT, THE *Q* IS DELIVERING TO YOU
A NOVEL ENTIRE, AND THIS IS JUST THE FIRST OF WHAT
THREATENS TO BECOME A HABIT. OR CALL IT A PRACTICE.
AT ALL EVENTS, BE IMPRESSED, PLEASE, WITH HOW WE
PROVE WILLING TO GET OUR PAGES ALL SHOVED OUT
OF PLACE JUST TO MAKE AN AMPLE SPACE FOR WHAT CANNOT
BE DENIED—THE WHICH IS, JUST TO BEGIN WITH, *GLASS*.
AND THE WHICH WILL FURTHER BE, COME *Q22*,
LAURA MARELLO'S *THE TENANTS OF THE HÔTEL BIRON*,
A NOVEL ANY MUCH AMPLER THAN WHICH EVEN WE,
IN OUR ROBUST ROOM-MAKING, COULD NOT POSSIBLY MANAGE.

## First, Harris

As the demographics of San Francisco's Castro District fluctuate dramatically under the dual impact of the AIDS epidemic and the on-going hemorrhage of refugees from the provinces, two distinct tiers of gay men have separated like oil and water out of this teeming multitude. First, there is the old clone, a dinosaur from the seventies whose near extinction has left a debilitated race of menopausal curiosities embalmed in their antiquated fetishes, bulging in leather chaps, their butts spilling out of the open flaps in the back like Play-Doh squished through a mold. Frozen in time by the devastating biological catastrophe that has turned this once flourishing community into a latter-day Pompeii, the older residents of the Castro seem so stunned by the injustice with which our innocent pastimes were brought to a halt that they muddle on like doddering veterans of war who refuse to take off their uniforms, wearing with patriotic pride the cowboy boots, the Stetsons, the halters, the cock rings—accoutrements that express defiance of our common enemy. Fenced off in the same ghetto with this group are the dinosaurs of the future, the new clones, androgynous boys in their twenties who seem to have been spliced from the same genetic strand of *haute couture*: tattered blue jeans ripped strategically to reveal patches of dingy undergarments clinging to delectable haunches, and leather jackets plastered with political convictions, with *de rigueur* bumper stickers that state explicitly (lest anyone think otherwise, given the less than formidable appearance of these harmless sylphs) that they are, as one sticker reads, "Militant Homosexual[s]." Spurning these emasculated twinkies, the old clones hate the new clones for refusing to respect the rules of precedence to which the old clones feel that they are so richly entitled as the dowagers of the gay movement, the subculture's unofficial aristocracy, men who hearken back to their illustrious political pedigree just as old soldiers reminisce about famous battles. The new clones, in turn, look contemptuously at these dispossessed relics clutching their heraldic shields to their breasts and condemn them as benighted assimilationists, as obedient fossils embedded in a subculture now thoroughly co-opted and commercialized. And yet in order to present a united front to protect ourselves from such frothing bigots as Helms and Dannemeyer, we nurse the illusion that the so-called "gay community" is characterized by peaceful solidarity when, in fact, simply to walk through the Castro is to run the gauntlet of generations divided by a yawning abyss of fashion, age, and attitude, the dizzying precipice on which gay rights often seem poised to plunge.

—DH

**THE**

**QUARTERLY**

To Ginny & Dale,
You are dears, always!

Love,
Emily

You loved it when we played catch with you

## Fractals, Bifurcations, Intermittencies and Periodicities, Folded-Towel Diffeomorphisms, Strange Attractors, Smooth-Noodle Maps, Accelerators, Recursions, and Songs of the Sea

The girl with the note that says Abalone Boulevard was born without a brain, which is very unusual. The babies without brains do not usually show up until you get farther out, like Perch Circle or Whitefish Road. It is especially unusual for a Jewish person, which this girl certainly is, though only by half-luck. *Which* half this actually is (read: who, in fact, is responsible) is the subject of an altogether different tale, which begins, for your pleasure, on another page. There will be no diversions here—in deference to the girl who was born without a brain and therefore totally incapable of any winning sort of satisfying personal diversion herself at all. No, not from the moment of the great birthing squeezing, that tortured, pink movement down writhing, too-tight sleeve; an unhappy piglet in endless snake gullet; a pummeling; a dismissal; a forced evacuation; a first taste of coercion in a state of pre-gasp; motherlove wringing and wringing her out. No, not from the hanging-out-to-dry by the doctors, their rubbings of chin and cold hand manipulations, their pokings the most pleasant part of the scene. (See *doctors*, pages and pages of *doctors*.)

Dead, not dead, is the question they battered around outside her skull for days and days, her skull, her tiny skull, her tiny, pink, beribboned skull. Empty. Alas. No hope for survival. No prospects for marriage. No potential love of farce. Dead, not dead, they posed to the philosophers who were called in from another emergency down the road. Dead, not dead, is all the same to me, said the woman wringing woman-pink and gristle from a mop. Dead, not dead, is not a worthy question, said the metaphysician scrubbing up across the hall. Right you are, said the granny who bundled her up, this baby without a brain, this dainty mule-and-puker, this unfortunate creation the granny bundled up to run past waiting plumbers and other consultants to the bus. But dead, not dead, is the question that confronts her, this baby without a brain, yellow now, no longer pink, as she stands three years big on the corner of Scallop and Kingfish, a sea breeze filling the space behind her eyes, the Abalone note her only instruction.

Oh, Granny. Oh, my. Oh, where are the haunchy women? The saddle-hipped, the swaddlers, the cushy pillow-nappers, the shtuppers of nipple and pickle and thumb-sucks of wine? The broad, blinding swooshes of smothering comfort—crowding, clucking, smelling of chicken and dill and thin sour milk and thick yellow feet? Where are the marzipan limbs so solidly planted under wool-sway, fretted and bound with tight blue knots and yellowed strappings, inviting impossibly up and back and in to fleshy shelter? The place-keepers, the herring-breathed restorers of shadowy safety, the deeply-bosomed sha-sayers, the lifters into the light? The circle of them, where? In porch chairs? In trees? Hidden somewhere in needle click, in mewmew, in shnuffle? Do they snooze, forgetful, their necks freshly soaped, sitting somewhere in sunshine, heaving yeast—oh, beloved fragrant swellings, their flesh wanting kneading, wanting punching down and kneading and careful, quiet watching, a great breathing volume of woman-mother, shluffing, sharing crony heat to puff and to rise?

Oh, to have rescue!

Oh, to have, at least, a brain! To be born again with thought, the girl thinks, without, of course, thinking—squeezing her legs together, holding her pishy, breathing in brine. I am safe, at least, from the burden of nostalgia. I am not obliged to brood on my bereavements, irretrievables, on grannies dead and safeties past, sucky-nursies left dirt-sugared under a swing, the tassels of blankets too much twirled and long since burned, gone pink things, fine brown flushings, and other comforts no longer to be found in this world. I can concentrate instead on the fluid needs of my simple physical matter, the parts that are fated to be satisfied or die, and by extension, the resolution of the question, dead, not dead, right on Scallop Avenue, left on Kingfish Road. But brainlessly, she turns her eyes to sky, looking for salvation in the edematous flesh of clouds that look to her to be rising from beyond the farthest houses: here a heavy hip shouldering into arm-bundled breast, there a bumping of roundnesses, loafy unnameable parts . . . swelling, puffing, rising . . . . . . inflating, sufflating . . . . . . . expanding, distending . . . . . . . . . . ballooning into death bloat . . . . . . . . . . . . . dispersing into ether . . . . . . . . . . . . . . returning unto spirit . . . . . . . . . . . . . . . . . . . . absent . . . . . . . . . . . . . . . . . . . . . . . . . . . . . . . . . . . . . gone . . . . . . . . . . . . . . . . . . . . . . . . . . . . . . . . . . . . . . . . . . . . . . . . . . . . . . . . . . . . . . . . . . . . . . . . . . . . . . . . the sky an empty skull. (For explanatory notes, call me later at home.) Liquid warmth wicks down her socks and splashes on her shoes. Empty. Empty. Lost. Lost, concludes the girl born to sorrow. Is it to be this way until the end of time? she muses. Me the sorry object of the will of another's brain?

Oh, you sly puss. But of course she has a brain. And you knew it all along. You imagined it for yourself, without waiting for me. Without the help of scribbles, you conjured up this brain, this magnificent brain, this lovely, furrowed, plump thing, gray, but, by rights, pink, and pulsing away with the worthiest, the very loftiest cerebrations. You can think—why, you have thought—of a hundred explanations, of twists and doublings back and ironic diverications. You have cogitated back to your readings of the past, to your personal knowledge of nothingnesses, comparative anatomy, God. But if you think your reader's ruminations have any effect on the progress of this story, you, my friend, were born without a brain. You are nowhere, toots, but at the corner of Scallop and Kingfish. For an easier read, see back there, or see past that.

. . .

But what is going on inside her head, then, you ask? This lost, this orphaned, this abandoned without a brain? Is she not presenting issues of healthy import, musings that are more than merely directional, an observing mind, some expenditure of energy beyond instinct? Does she not think? What, exactly, you are asking, does brain provide?

Ahhhhhhhhhh.

Let me divert you with a parable.

### A PARABLE

Once there was a king who had, for head, a goldfish bowl, because all of the lands he admired were close beside the sea. He fished. He entered the waters on a pretense of ankle-bathing, of finding surcease in the susurrus, the endless summoning of waves. Oh, such sounds. How they bewitched him, rushing in around his feet and rising through his flesh in great, sonorous waves! Crash! Oh, crash again! he would shout across the water. I have found an infinity in sibilance, and a lully place between the sha la's. Sha la sha la. Ooolooloo. Sha la sha la. Ooolooloo. And he danced a great beside-the-sea dance, undulating, ululating, answering each surge and willing each swell to arc over him, engulf him, to fill his empty vessel—to teach his earth-bound waters the billow and cadence of ocean wisdom, to fill his glassy head with oh, such splendid shiny creatures: quick darts, all fin and bone; and the more meaty, deeper of sea; the mighty ponderous; the mere-pretties; the flamboyant; the self-concealed; entire, historic, well-integrated schools; the Leviathan too grand to be aquarium-accommodated; and the favorite of the king, the exuberant amoeba, dividing and dividing in oozy triumph over death.

They are in my head! They are in my head! I have dominion over all! And the king, in ocean-ecstasy, dove deep within himself, into the glass-bowl waters still heaving in sea-dance rhythm, dove in to consort with his capture, to become one with his friendly prey, never again to look out on a world that terrifies the brainless.

Weird, you say. But whose head are you swimming around in now?

So tell me I enthrall you. Tell me that you are my creature, that you love being here inside, that I can keep you here in this space behind my eyes, lifting you only as I please into the light. Sha la sha la. Oooloolooloo. Sha la sha la. Oooloolooloo. Shainy shainy zeisy shainy nubby nubby woo. Let me lull. Let me tell you all the inside lies.

Here the king interrupts with plot turns of a certain lusty elegance. Thank God for the king. (See *God*.) (See *king*.)

(See *plot*.)

Doctors! Doctors! Doctors! Doctors! Doctors! Doctors!
Doctors! Doctors! Doctors! Doctors! Doctors! Doctors!
Doctors! Doctors! Doctors! Doctors! Doctors! Doctors!
Doctors! Doctors! Doctors! Doctors! Doctors! Doctors!
Doctors! Doctors! Doctors! Doctors! Doctors! Doctors!
Doctors! Doctors! Doctors! Doctors! Doctors! Doctors!
Doctors! Doctors! Doctors! Doctors! Doctors! Doctors!
Doctors! Doctors! Doctors! Doctors! Doctors! Doctors!
Doctors! Doctors! Doctors! Doctors! Doctors! Doctors!
Doctors! Doctors! Doctors! Doctors! Doctors! Doctors!
Doctors! Doctors! Doctors! Doctors! Doctors! Doctors!
Doctors! Doctors! Doctors! Doctors! Doctors! Doctors!
Doctors! Doctors! Doctors! Doctors! Doctors! Doctors!
Doctors! Doctors! Doctors! Doctors! Doctors! Doctors!
Doctors! Doctors! Doctors! Doctors! Doctors! Doctors!

Doctors! Doctors! Doctors! Doctors! Doctors! Doctors!
Doctors! Doctors! Doctors! Doctors! Doctors! Doctors!
Doctors! Doctors! Doctors! Doctors! Doctors! Doctors!
Doctors! Doctors! Doctors! Doctors! Doctors! Doctors!
Doctors! Doctors! Doctors! Doctors! Doctors! Doctors!
Doctors! Doctors! Doctors! Doctors! Doctors! Doctors!
Doctors! Doctors! Doctors! Doctors! Doctors! Doctors!
Doctors! Doctors! Doctors! Doctors! Doctors! Doctors!
Doctors! Doctors! Doctors! Doctors! Doctors! Doctors!
Doctors! Doctors! Doctors! Doctors! Doctors! Doctors!
Doctors! Doctors! Doctors! Doctors! Doctors! Doctors!
Doctors! Doctors! Doctors! Doctors! Doctors! Doctors!
Doctors! Doctors! Doctors! Doctors! Doctors! Doctors!
Doctors! Doctors! Doctors! Doctors! Doctors! Doctors!
Doctors! Doctors! Doctors! Doctors! Doctors! Doctors!
Doctors! Doctors! Doctors! Doctors! Doctors! Doctors!
Doctors! Doctors! Doctors! Doctors! Doctors! Doctors!
Doctors! Doctors! Doctors! Doctors! Doctors! Doctors!
Doctors! Doctors! Doctors! Doctors! Doctors! Doctors!
Doctors! Doctors! Doctors! Doctors! Doctors! Doctors!
Doctors! Doctors! Doctors! Doctors! Doctors! Doctors!
Doctors! Doctors! Doctors! Doctors! Doctors! Doctors!
Doctors! Doctors! Doctors! Doctors! Doctors! Doctors!
Doctors! Doctors! Doctors! Doctors! Doctors! Doctors!
Doctors! Doctors! Doctors! Doctors! Doctors! Doctors!
Doctors! Doctors! Doctors! Doctors! Doctors! Doctors!
Doctors! Doctors! Doctors! Doctors! Doctors! Doctors!
Doctors! Doctors! Doctors! Doctors! Doctors! Doctors!
Doctors! Doctors! Doctors! Doctors! Doctors! Doctors!
Doctors! Doctors! Doctors! Doctors! Doctors! Doctors!
Doctors! Doctors! Doctors! Doctors! Doctors! Doctors!
Doctors! Doctors! Doctors! Doctors! Doctors! Doctors!
Doctors! Doctors! Doctors! Doctors! Doctors! Doctors!
Doctors! Doctors! Doctors! Doctors! Doctors! Doctors!

Doctors! Doctors! Doctors! Doctors! Doctors! Doctors!
Doctors! Doctors! Doctors! Doctors! Doctors! Doctors!
Doctors! Doctors! Doctors! Doctors! Doctors! Doctors!
Doctors! Doctors! Doctors! Doctors! Doctors! Doctors!
Doctors! Doctors! Doctors! Doctors! Doctors! Doctors!
Doctors! Doctors! Doctors! Doctors! Doctors! Doctors!
Doctors! Doctors! Doctors! Doctors! Doctors! Doctors!
Doctors! Doctors! Doctors! Doctors! Doctors! Doctors!
Doctors! Doctors! Doctors! Doctors! Doctors! Doctors!
Doctors! Doctors! Doctors! Doctors! Doctors! Doctors!
Doctors! Doctors! Doctors! Doctors! Doctors! Doctors!
Doctors! Doctors! Doctors! Doctors! Doctors! Doctors!
Doctors! Doctors! Doctors! Doctors! Doctors! Doctors!
Doctors! Doctors! Doctors! Doctors! Doctors! Doctors!
Doctors! Doctors! Doctors! Doctors! Doctors! Doctors!
Doctors! Doctors! Doctors! Doctors! Doctors! Doctors!
Doctors! Doctors! Doctors! Doctors! Doctors! Doctors!
Doctors! Doctors! Doctors! Doctors! Doctors! Doctors!
Doctors! Doctors! Doctors! Doctors! Doctors! Doctors!
Doctors! Doctors! Doctors! Doctors! Doctors! Doctors!
Doctors! Doctors! Doctors! Doctors! Doctors! Doctors!
Doctors! Doctors! Doctors! Doctors! Doctors! Doctors!
Doctors! Doctors! Doctors! Doctors! Doctors! Doctors!
Doctors! Doctors! Doctors! Doctors! Doctors! Doctors!
Doctors! Doctors! Doctors! Doctors! Doctors! Doctors!
Doctors! Doctors! Doctors! Doctors! Doctors! Doctors!
Doctors! Doctors! Doctors! Doctors! Doctors! Doctors!
Doctors! Doctors! Doctors! Doctors! Doctors! Doctors!
Doctors! Doctors! Doctors! Doctors!

Have I lost you? Oh, God! Oh, would that I had!
Oh, would that I had lost us both. In endless diversion and
lullabation, in brainless pages, elliptical fits. In tales of
fishes and mops and kings, of pink distractions and salty
air. In shilly shally shoo, in woolums, wollums, woo.

A dillydally dawdle before the last blank page. Q

## Piggy Among the Elders

The sugar cone cartons came on Mondays.

A truck brought them. A man from the truck's cabin came around to the rear of the truck, opened the rear, slid the cartons forward on the truck's platform—one of them, two of them, three of them. You'd have thought every sugar cone in those cartons would have broken, the way the man had tossed them from the platform.

The man unloading the truck touched his hand to the trellis that ran along the pilings of the club. A section of the trellis came off on his hand—it seemed that way. Ice comes off on your hand that way when the ice is so cold that it burns. And out from the place where the trellis board had been removed came a person, the thick-lipped boy who worked around the club.

The boxes were loaded, one of them, two of them, three of them, onto the steel dolly owned by the club. The thick-lipped boy made Piggy think that the boy's lips had been made by being slashed by window-glass.

Piggy and Tuna Man and Sam the Salami Man made their way down the tunnel that led to the innards of the club. They made their way quickly. Scurrying, you might say. They clung to the wall of the tunnel.

Piggy and Sam the Salami Man and Tuna Man slipped into the shadow of where, on one side of the tunnel, the wall turned. Then they took a turn into a deeper shade.

Mildewed beach umbrellas were what they saw when their eyes adjusted to the darkness. And a stack of bleached-from-red kickboards.

. . .

Piggy and Sam the Salami Man and Tuna Man began again down the tunnel. They took a turn, and then a turn, and then another turn. They stood staring into the blackness they found there. They understood, though: the darkness has a way of seeping out of things.

They waited.

A slat of light appeared.

Turned slowly into the edge of a shutter, a pile of shutters.

Now down by their feet they saw a saltine wrapper. A little farther on, an enormous rubber glove.

Their eyes were drawn not once but twice, and then again, Piggy's were, and Tuna's were, and Sam the Salami Man's were too, to the suitcase-sized square of constant dripping to the side of them.

Piggy and Sam the Salami Man and Tuna Man pulled themselves into a slit of darkness.

They did so on their elbows.

Their legs dragging uselessly behind them.

Stop!

Rats as large as sand sharks could have been nosing around with them! And shards of glass could have been there! And nails that lay as they fell, pointed end up—the look-out! tips of Piggy's mother's peony, her platycodon. Panties were being taken down in there, indeed!—fireflies! fireflies!—if they could only get to them—those white flashes happening up over them.

But Piggy and Sam the Salami Man and Tuna Man had got no farther into that sandy slit of darkness than the illuminated blue rim of the locker boy's pants—that was all they would have seen had they turned over in there. And I can tell you that just getting yourself to turn over in that crawl space is a day's work. It's like having to turn the whole woman of the place over on top of you, turning your face up into the floorboards, losing sight of the sand that is beneath you.

. . .

Piggy stood squinting in the sunlight in the truck unloading zone.

Piggy held two bits of information tightly in his mind.

There was an opening about yea-high up in the concrete wall of the tunnel; he had seen it. There was a cardboard box somewhere down the tunnel; he had seen that, too. He held these bits of information to himself. He held them the way one holds to oneself the notion of the girl one might like to start going after.

The cardboard box was a heavy-sided one, a liquor box. It had a damp top to it that would have collapsed had Piggy stood on it in the center. That's the sort you're apt to find lying around in places where the dampness seems to seed itself everywhere.

Piggy got up on the box, placing his feet on the box's edges. The box brought him eye-level with the opening in the concrete wall.

The sand in that opening rose and fell in the shape of grave mounds. Teardrop sun stones were scattered across it—mysteriously formed ovals of light about the size of a woman's fingernails; and an odd pile of thin black combs was just to the side of where Piggy first peered in.

Nudged through the floorboards from above.

Not that the oddness of those combs being there, all in one place, did then, nor would it ever after that, touch Piggy's mind.

Piggy hoisted himself into the space.

Piggy had no sooner drawn himself fully into there when he saw a flash of orange just above him. Oh, lucky boy that he was! It was like letting your hook down and right away having a fish on it!

It made his heart jump.

Right beside the orange, Piggy saw an eyeball.

. . .

Piggy and Sam the Salami Man and Tuna Man hoisted themselves one at a time up through the opening in the concrete wall of the tunnel. First Piggy. Then Sam the Salami Man. Then Tuna Man.

Nails, spiderwebs, broken and whole Coca-Cola bottles were in there. The Coca-Cola bottles were glass, real glass.

Quick! They heard a noise.

They scrambled over to where they thought the noise was coming from, hardened into place under an old man's voice.

"Five. Two. Eight," they heard, their mouths and eyes made round by nothing more than the old man's saying his numbers, the shuffling of his feet dusting so fine a dusting of sand down over them—it was like powdered sugar, almost— too fine to make them even close their mouths.

Piggy and Sam the Salami Man and Tuna Man had dyed their shorts in tea-stained water. The shorts had come out flesh-colored and wrinkly—like the backs of women's legs. They had made other preparations too, equally useless.

Piggy and Sam the Salami Man and Tuna Man heard footsteps.

Footsteps going to the string that was hanging from the floorboards of Piggy's locker, for they had set a bit of kite string hanging there.

A string to get their bearings from.

"That might be my mom," Piggy said.

"That might be my mom, Tuna," Piggy said again—after he had caught up to where Tuna Man had already crawled to, this time grabbing the slab of Tuna Man's shoulder. "Hey," he said, "that might be my mom!"

There was a silence.

"Yeah," said Tuna Man.

"Yeah," said Sam the Salami Man.

Although neither Tuna Man nor Sam the Salami Man

moved in the lecturelike pause of another little bit of silence that Piggy did not like listening to. And then they all heard the blessing of Mr. Van Dyne calling, "Ned! Ned!" which was the name of the thick-lipped boy who transported the cartons of sugar cones back through the tunnel. "Ned, are you all right in there?" they heard, which set them scurrying out of there, even though the voice was sand valleys and dark nights away from them and they were safe.

Let me describe this to you. Have you ever seen those paintings of the martyrs? Well, that's how Piggy and Sam the Salami Man and Tuna Man lay under there, the three of them as still as the figures in a flat painted tableau are, one of them pointing—white-chinned, wide-eyed—at the ribs of the floor-boards.

"It smells like beef broth," they heard.

"Touch it again. It does."

"Seedlings," Sam the Salami Man said, by which he meant not sisters but younger sisters, referring to the way their beavers were just hairless little y-shaped things at the bottom of their bellies. And here's another one—privet hedges, which was short for in-the-shade privet hedges, which was short for those old ladies who have just scraggly things.

As if that part of them had never seen sunlight.

Piggy and Tuna Man and Sam the Salami Man pulled themselves to half-sitting positions, sipped from their drinks, and lay themselves on their backs again. Feet with shoes on them announced themselves down the thin blue pinstripes of the aisles between the lockers. Pants with belt buckles in them knocked against the arms of locker chairs and on floorboards. The knocks startled Piggy and Sam the Salami Man and Tuna Man. It was their fathers who were here today, their fathers who had got them drinks from the bar—purple transfusions, bright-red grenadine drinks.

A noise!

Piggy and Tuna Man and Sam the Salami Man were over to where they thought the noise was—shoulder-ruddering their way to the length of string that they'd set hanging from the McPartlands' locker, using their bent knees to motor with silently.

A lot of white came in along with Mrs. McPartland.

"It's the nurse," Tuna Man whispered to Piggy. "They're going to milk."

"You don't think she can fucking hear you?" Sam the Salami Man said.

"Righto, Mrs. Garter," a man's voice said.

Then Tuna Man found himself looking straight into the eyeball of the man—the white of it, the hammer-struck blue of it, the stone-black of it.

Those eyes are no more able to see down where you are than the eyes of the dead are.

Tit! Piggy and Tuna Man and Sam the Salami Man were thinking. Tit!

Piggy and Tuna Man and Sam the Salami Man aligned and realigned themselves under Mrs. McPartland. But all they could see was Mrs. McPartland's hand webbing the baby's head, and Mrs. McPartland's toes, which were glowing around the edges, as if a flashlight were shining through them.

Piggy and Tuna Man and Sam the Salami Man had caught one sister. She stood so still before the two dark knobs that marked where the bureau was that Piggy and Tuna Man and Sam the Salami Man had time to motor over to her and arrange themselves under her; so still, in fact, that they lay listless and every-which-way pointed as fish when they have nothing to fin around for, or soldiers felled in battle lying face-up staring, so still that all three of them knew what she was doing up there—picking her pimples—although none of them—not Piggy or Tuna Man or Sam the Salami Man—each afraid of exposing the means by which he had come upon this knowledge—said as much, not until later when they had swum out to her in the ocean—oh, how the cold of that water makes your wounds cry out at you, your new wounds and your old wounds, too.

Piggy and Tuna Man and Sam the Salami Man were lying belly-down on the sand beneath the floorboards.

"But my mom's ugly," Tuna Man said.

They were lying in the configuration of a tripod.

"My mom's so ugly," Tuna said, "that her ass hangs on her back like a pair of elephant ears, and her tits hang the same way down her front."

"Shut up, for Christ's sake," Sam the Salami Man said.

But what was passing was another flash of younger sisters, which Piggy and Sam the Salami Man and Tuna Man could tell by the patches of darkness that passed by off to the side of them as swift as windy little clouds.

"My mom's no better than a two-bib baby," Tuna Man said. Then Tuna Man added—as if no amount of detail concerning his mother's ugliness could ever be sufficient to describe it—"The mere sight of my mom would make you puke in your kneeholes. That's how ugly she is," Tuna Man said, moving to show Piggy and Sam the Salami Man the holes in the sand that his knees had made.

Not that scratchings and scrapings and other such noises were not going on above them.

But Piggy and Sam the Salami Man and Tuna Man hardly ever moved toward noises any more. Or away from noises, either. They were tired, after all, all three of them were, of waiting under nobody's locker, or anybody's locker, or lockers where there were only six-year-olds who sat around all morning on one locker bench or another locker bench, whispering and showing of themselves nothing but the airborne flicks, common as pigeons, of their feet. If you had spent as much time under the floorboards of the lockers as Piggy had and Sam the Salami Man had and Tuna Man had, you would have felt that even the sand down by the sea—dense as that sand was—must have had passageways under it, and slots that could be seen up from.

Piggy and Sam the Salami Man and Tuna Man had given up.

It might have looked that way.

Piggy and Tuna Man were sitting on the terrace of the club, concerning themselves with the lukewarm drippings that came from the bottoms of their ice-cream cones.

With catching those drippings on their tongues.

Sam the Salami Man was slumped under an umbrella down by the entrance to the lockers—Sam the Salami Man, whose own mother had been incapable of eating anything, not even ice cream, some two or three months now—the Virgin Mary, Sam the Salami Man called her, for the fact that Mary was her name and for the fact that no one could have touched her, not anyone—although Piggy and Tuna Man could see the vice she still held Sam the Salami Man in, or that her brain eaten by maggots did, or whatever had eaten her out and scooped her down to a freakish thing—nothing left on her anywhere but the tip of her beaver; so ugly—and she no more than forty—that you'd let your ice cream melt into milk in your mouth if you had to sit faced the way she was faced.

Lift it a little?

Just to look?

Oh, life's no coil of sweets, my boys—that's not what's down there.

But never mind, for here she comes, sooner than Piggy or Tuna Man or even Sam the Salami Man had expected, or that I had expected either—Piggy's mom, that's who, making her way up the stone steps—she's skipped a step, she's young, you see—one never takes into account a thing like that when one's so young oneself. She's approaching Mr. Van Dyne—Mr. Van Dyne where he sits at the top of the steps, his fingers poised to push the pad for signing-in guests into the proper position for right- or left-handers, depending upon who he sees coming.

Piggy's mom passes Mr. Van Dyne. He nods his clipped nod to her—he's impervious to her charms. And she nods to him, too, not pausing—no guest she!—striding from there down the colonnaded walk of window boxes overflowing with ageratum, impatiens—if it had been September, she'd have been shooing Piggy away from snapping the seed pods of those plants, and from dropping hairy-legged caterpillars into plastic bar cups.

Too old for that? Do you think Piggy really is?

Striding past the lifeguard, now she is—the lifeguard who sets his legs straight out in front of him, resting on their ankles as if his legs were made of wood.

There were no friends for Piggy's mom to wave to, or to pause to talk to—not that day; that day was an empty, weekday day, by all accounts—the emptiness of which drew her quick into the lockers.

Go back to it one more time: Piggy's mom's legs heading straight for under the arch that leads to the lockers. Sam the Salami Man off to give his signal. Piggy, Tuna Man, and Sam the Salami Man going for it across the bricks, out to the truck unloading zone, into where under the lockers is.

Here is, more or else, how it happened.

"Who's coming?" Piggy asked.

"Cunt is cunt," Sam the Salami Man said. "Who cares who's coming?" said Sam the Salami Man. "So what if it's your mom?"

Then the three of them are into position fast under the floorboards of Piggy's locker, waiting on their backs as if they had just been strapped into the Zipper at the Firemen's Carnival, Piggy having chosen a chin-sized dip of sand to rest his head in, the floorboards over him being somewhat widely set apart there and somewhat rotted.

A man makes choices even if he has no notion of the why and wherefore of them. There's that to be considering.

Footsteps are coming down the aisle. Footsteps stop. A key squeaks in the darkened copper lock of the locker door. Sandals make their bang and clap on the locker floor. A beach bag makes the soft sound of being set on the seat of the canvas-seated chair. Then came the sound of what must have been a kicked-off sandal, for there was the sound of something hard as a heel hitting wood, and Tuna Man began pushing his head aimlessly in the sand.

"She's over here!" Tuna Man was whispering.

"Shit, she is," Sam the Salami Man said. "She's here!" for just then had come the softer sound of something like a pant leg lassoing down on itself, and the back of Sam the Salami Man's skull had gone to rooting, too.

Oh, there were some pretty parts, to be sure.

Piggy and Tuna Man and Sam the Salami Man arranged in the pale rosette of their unsummered flesh and the light that made them sand-colored. Piggy lying face-up with his eyes shut and his hands clasped over his chest without his knowing that on his chest was where his arms were.

Piggy was praying.

Piggy was praying that his mother's feet were fast, getting in and out of clothes. He was praying that his mother's skin was smooth. He was praying that his mother's breasts were white and uplifted.

Which made Piggy think of the tips on soft ice creams.

Piggy winced.

Piggy opened his eyes.

The big pink plate of Piggy's mother was over him.

It was a bumpy mass rearranging itself in globules.

A long black crack that was sure to be the butt crack smoothed itself out over Piggy without revealing beaver.

Piggy was eyeballs, heartbeat, mouth—nothing else was.

Suddenly he realized—Jesus! he was looking right at it,

he'd almost missed it, it was—Jesus, yes it was!—the hole, the hair, the unpink color—it was everything that beaver was. Get out with what he'd got! Get out with what he'd got! That was the thing to be urging him; but, good God! he couldn't—for there was another thing that rose above him, a thing too terrible to touch, a thing that had been there all this time, fully rendered all this time, and he not knowing it. It took his breath away. It made his heart pound. Oh, Jesus, what was the first? A start in the wrong place? A thing that fell from this other's being made?

Take the first! Take the first!

But his mind dropped the crinkly-edged penny he had found first. Dropped it for this second thing. This thing that was rending the darkness, that was as dark as the darkness, that was flesh scored and scored again. That was fetid, serrated, looming up over him, leering at him with its lippy malicious leer and laughing at him down there helpless, he and his little bit of change he'd just about made off with.

And so close!

So close that with his tongue it seemed he could have almost touched it!

Draw back a bit now, please.

No need to see, smell, taste what Piggy did.

It splatted on Piggy's eyes, on Piggy's mouth.

Piggy tasted the shoots of it, the splintering of it.

No drinking from it! Not you! Not you! Not you!

"She's pissing, man. Let's get out of here," Sam the Salami Man said.

Not that the stream of it lasted long. In fact, the stream of it was such that anyone but an old man, or an old woman, or a young child, could have held it off from coming.

Oh, what a careless thing a woman is, pissing in the place she pisses in, just for the place's being there, not even looking to see what it is she's pissing on, no more than a stupid rabbit, on top its own shadow, looks to see; and, oh, what a pity for Piggy as he lay there—his brain mostly darkness, his candy-ass stuck there, his relentless voice ordering him on up elsewhere.

A bit of poetry, my boys, a bit of poetry.

Oh, sometimes I see Piggy long after Tuna Man and Sam the Salami Man have scurried off from there—his lips shut tight, his mind stuck open.

Or I see Piggy on hands and knees up in his locker, wiping his mother's urine up with a towel he found up there and crying like a whore. He's devising, even as he cries, how he'll go back to them, to Sam the Salami Man and to Tuna Man.

If you can imagine any way out of the spot that Piggy found himself in, that was how he got out of it.

Perhaps nothing ever happened to Piggy that was worse. Perhaps nothing ever happened to Piggy that was better.

On the other hand, if that's the worst that might happen to a man, he'll die a lucky man—you could say that, too, and not be wrong.

Oh, it will put the hair on your chests, and on your chins; and on your chins and on your chins, and make it sprout there, too, and black as you could want it.

Go to it, boys! Put your tongue to it, put your heart to it, put your mind to it. Lick it, bite it, suck it, crunch it. Oh, eat it if you can, eat it to the creamy tip of it. Eat it to the stone-cold clit of it. **Q**

## Glass

I

Eddie Niijls' landlord comes by and says the building is being sold, and anyone not out by the end of the month will be evicted.

Eddie looks at his landlord's tie. All small dots.

—I know this is a hardship.

—I thought they gave you a tax break, Eddie says.

—Right, Ed, *gave*. Public-private partnership, place for the arts, they ran us all around the track.

—I thought—

—We had hopes, and we got shit. Privatization is the coming thing. They brought it down. I've got to live.

Eddie's dealer, George, calls and tells Eddie to stop by the gallery. Eddie considers his situation. He has, maybe, eight hundred bucks. A beautiful day. He watches a woman on a bicycle. She wears a spandex suit. Panels of color on the black. Fall season: geometrics. Bright rectangles. Mondrian.

Spray paint on a garage wall. X'd out. Triangles? Stars? Symbols.

Work in the streets. Guys started that way. Subways.

Eddie sees a bronze in the gallery. Three fused triangles. Smallest to largest. The largest eleven inches by eleven inches by eleven inches.

Like a miniature public piece.

Clean in a way.

Eddie does not recognize the artist's name.

Triangles.

—You are not moving forward, George says.

—So you dump me?

—A painter stalls, then comes back stronger.

—Come over and see what I'm doing.

George says he will be over in a few days.

Eddie calls around to see if anybody knows of a building with spacious flats that belongs to a widow who has not raised the rent in the years since her husband's death. Eddie's friends have heard of the place, but they are not sure where it is.

He needs to work. He has seventeen days. People move all the time.

Eddie goes into the spare room. His studio. No skylight, but there is a glass balcony door and a row of windows. As good light as can be got. Eddie takes a two-foot-by-two-foot sheet of quarter-inch plywood from the stack on the floor, sets it on the sawhorse table, and gives it a coat of cheap house paint. He does another. Another.

George says he will come around 3:oo. Eddie cleans the place up. He sets the painting up in the spare room, then moves it to the living room. He puts the picture on a straight chair and places the desk lamp on the floor so its light shines on the canvas. He would like to hang the piece. That might be too much. George sees work rough every day.

Eddie has espresso, Chinese beer, wine. George is late. Eddie walks in circles.

George enters apologizing.

—You want a beer or something?

—Thanks, no time. Let's work.

Eddie motions toward the light. —This is the first in a series.

Aluminum gray background. The words:

FEAR BRAZIL

DESIRE BERLIN

DEATH TAHITI

arranged in block letters.

—It is over, George says. Finished.

—But—

—Too concept. Too done.

—Uh—

—Maybe ten years ago. Maybe.

—Well—

—Now it's the sex thing. Get on board.

—Sex?

—Bodies. Or at least shapes. Curves, for Christ's sake.

Eddie cannot afford the same square footage. He checks the want ads. Looks at half a side-by-side duplex. Busted-up picket fence. Plywood over the basement windows. Thanks, no. Bodies. Curves. Ragged line of spray paint on the dirty wall. Break it up. Juxtaposed vertical lines. UPC.

I I

They come in a blast. Eddie crouches, hands before his face. The sun bright. Spandexed figures part as they fly past on roller blades.

—Bicycle trail, one yells.

Eddie sees the sign, moves from the tarmac to the sidewalk. Lake and ribbon of dirty sand—the nominal beach—to his right. By the waters of Calhoun. He steps around a thin young man who is carrying a cane. That back?

Look. Light breaking through the trees. Sail boats and sail boards contending on the water, neat triangles above fiberglass bases. Runners pass. Bronze flesh. Health.

Harps hanging in the trees. The angel of the Lord appears in the raiment of fire and glory to divide the multitudes—swimmers from sailors, skaters from joggers, sick from healthy—and dispense the awesome justice of the divine.

In the raiment of pure light.

Beer bottle. Clear. Mexican. Our friend glass.

He gets home. Number 103. The constant pressure of money. A fifteen-by-fifteen-foot efficiency with kitchenette and midget bath. Somebody painted the wooden floor. Scarred now. Canvas tacked to the sawhorse and plywood table. Only two windows. Hundred-watt bulbs in every fixture and three trouble lights hanging from nails.

Footsteps. The postman lugs his bag of despair.

Nothing falls through the slot.

Perhaps tomorrow.

Three hours til he has to be at work.

The supervisor bought his story. —Returning student, okay. Waxing experience?

He has floors six and eight. Office cleaning. Nice to look at the individual touches in the cubicles. Calendars. Mugs. Cartoons.

Twenty hours a week. Covers the groceries and electric bill. With his savings.

Among the women at work, a woman. Eddie is taken by her hair. By her face. Body. Presence. Dolores. She has her story.

Eddie has trouble sleeping. The future plays out before him.

Four-wheel drive in the parking lot. Chief Cherokee. Decorative strip on the side. Navaho pattern.

Kid from the janitorial service walks up. —Need something?

—I like the design.

The kid has a crinkly scar like a vaccination mark on his cheek.

He points to it. —A guy shot me.

He holds up his hand. Another scar. —Here too.

—Got to roll, Eddie says. See you.

A man with a video camera takes Eddie's picture.

He tries stencils. Repeated patterns. The alphabet.

. . .

George looks fit.
—Lose some weight?
—No, no. I'm on a new program.
—Seems to be working for you.
—I think so; perhaps I flatter myself.

The ex-husband was a weapons enthusiast. They
would go shooting on weekends. Drive to a gravel pit. Other
people shot there. Couples. Families.

—Come for a drink, George says.
—Well—
—Don't beg off.
The bar. Clean. Sunlight on the polished wood, brass and
porcelain tap handles.
—Dry martini, no olive.
Beer. Tap is cheaper. George will pick it up. Imports.

He went to weapon collectors' shows. Hobby. But
what he brought home. Swords. Maces. A suit of armor, the
whole thing. He had always liked fantasy books. Began to talk
about torture.

Neat bottle with harp. 355 milliliters.
—Let's not waste time, George says.
—What's your story?
—What's your gripe?
—Why blame me?

He would not answer the door. Left guns and ammu-
nition all over the place. Quit working. Would not go out.
When she left, he shook his head and said, you too?
She would call. He would never answer.

. . .

—Lone wolf, starvation, George says. Save it for the movie. Anyway, I'm bought out. Company got me, corporation got them. Remember the pictures of the food chain in your sixth grade science book? The fish?

The printer's sign is mounted on a steel reinforcing rod:

PRINTING
WEDDING INVITATIONS
BUSINESS FORMS
CARDS
NOTARY PUBLIC
STAMPS MADE

A tall man. Bald. Stooped among the yellowed samples. Requesting the pleasure of your presence. Manager of sales. Small black press a dinosaur of science and industry. The printer's unsettling eyes like dull marbles in the skull.

—It won't be long, he says.

She got worried about him. It seemed normal that he would not answer the phone until she realized how abnormal that was. She wanted to be sure he was all right. He could have been dead. Suicide. Or hurt himself while he was drunk and bled to death in the bathroom.

Her brother went along to warn her if there was something she should not see.

Her ex was sitting on the floor with a circle of guns around him: rifles, pistols, shotguns. Pint of whiskey in one hand. Empty tallboys scattered about.

He went for a revolver. Slipped out of his hand, fell on the shag carpet. Grabbed it. Slipped again. Hand on the walnut grips. He mumbled.

She was afraid it would go off.

Told him it was her. Told him everything was okay.

. . .

—The last I heard he was in California in a cooperative living situation.
—A commune?
—They don't use that word.
—One big house?
—They have four or five townhouses.

Eddie pushes a cart through the halls, filling it with trash bags. He goes to the basement.
The incinerator man mumbles.
Eddie takes an empty cart.
—Burn the syringes, the incinerator man says.

The printer's teeth a twisted muddle.
—Custom stamp.
—How much?
—Seventeen even. What do you do?
—I'm an artist.
—You don't see that much nowadays.

—Have another, George says. Maybe a snack? By the way, describe every feeling you've ever experienced: emotional, psychological, physical.

The stamp makes a neat black Uzi.

—He makes things, George says. I sell things.
—Past and future.
—Simple.

—Practice evasion, George says.

Bordered by the crossed black Uzis, the architecture of landscaping, trimmed hedges and shaped trees, flower beds outlined in plastic pipe. The flagstones of the walk are sharp, but muted in tone. They lead to the cedar walls and paneled doors of the townhouses. Perspective is perfect, the clarity almost superreal. An orange tree dominates the foreground, its ripe fruit shining in the sun.

—Be someone else, George says.

III

The Concealment Artist walks onto the stage. The auditorium is dark, the audience silent. It is hard to tell, from the seats below the stage, the size of the man. Well-proportioned, yes, but tall or short is impossible to say. His clothing is undistinguished: jeans, sweatshirt, corduroy sports coat, desert boots. His hair is brown. He is clean-shaven.

—All names are aliases, he says, to sparse laughter, the odd clap and whistle.

—Where's the screen? Eddie says.

—What? says Dolores.

—Isn't there a video?

—I don't know. My sister won the tickets. I thought you'd like it.

The stage is barren except for a velvet-covered stand. A woman, blonde, muscled, attractive in a huge and theatrical way in her spangled magician's assistant's suit, brings the weapons to the table. They shine—the steel mini-derringer, the chrome twenty-five auto, the ten-shot twenty-two semi, the stainless thirty-eight special, the chopped forty-five, the full-sized wonder nine—all laid out like toys beneath a Christmas tree. She goes behind the curtains, reappears with a wooden easel, and places a poster on it. A musical flourish from the 1890's plays. The poster says CONCEALMENT ARTIST. Scattered applause. The man on stage bows. Raises his hands. The sleeves of his jacket fall away from his forearms, exposing vague tattoos.

—My background is best left to the imagination, the artist says. As are all of ours.

He twists, turns, spirals. The guns disappear. Enter two men in police uniforms. The artist places his hands palms down on the stand, bends forward.

One policeman draws his revolver and holds it on the artist. The other policeman frisks the artist, comes up empty-handed. The policemen switch roles. The second cop finds nothing. Applause. The artist bows.

The woman brings out a unicycle. The artist mounts to applause. He goes forward and backward, stands on the pedals, almost flips. No weapon falls. He leaps like a ballerina, lands tiptoed on the seat of the rolling unicycle. It is only an instant, but the effect seems longer. He hops off, bows, and flips into a series of quick cartwheels around the stage.

While he towels off with a silk scarf, the spangled lady pushes a safe on stage. She handcuffs the artist and pushes him inside. His head sticks out through a hole in the top. She cuts the safe, and apparently the artist, in half with an acetylene torch and wheels the lower half of the safe around the stage. The upper half hangs fixed in the air. The artist's eyes follow the progress of the lower half. His head and the top of the safe spin slowly, then quickly. The woman places the lower half beneath the upper half. The upper half drops slowly, still spinning, and screws itself onto the lower half. The artist's head disappears into the safe. He pops the door open and leaps out, free of the handcuffs.

The woman sets up a card table and two folding chairs and exits center stage. The Concealment Artist sits down. A screen drops from the ceiling. A picture of the President is projected on the screen. The Concealment Artist stands. The picture changes. Now it is a senator.

The artist stands in the light of the projection. He strikes the eighteen martial postures. The projector shuts down. The theater is pitch black. Eddie coughs. Someone answers with a faraway cough. Silence. The lights come up.

Eddie finds himself on stage. He scans the audience but

cannot see beyond the third row. Dolores is lost to him. The lights are hotter than he imagined. The Concealment Artist looms large. He is gigantic, six-four or five with upper arms as big as Eddie's thighs and hands like cafeteria trays. He invites Eddie to frisk him. Eddie gives him a perfunctory patting down, hands trembling.

The audience giggles. The artist says something Eddie does not catch. The giggles become a roar of laughter. The artist pushes Eddie to a folding chair. Eddie sits at the card table. The artist walks center stage. The lights go down; a spot hits the artist. Eddie looks at the vinyl table top. It is torn and has been patched with a piece of duct tape. He looks up—dark, empty space. The artist produces the pistols, beginning with the forty-five and working his way down to the humble mini-derringer. Each comes out of his clothes easily, naturally, with a little flourish of his hand. Burst of applause.

Eddie cannot help but be a little amazed. True, his frisk was not much, but he clearly passed his hands over some of the guns without feeling them. The woman looks as though she has been gilded—a walking statue—until Eddie realizes she is wearing a gold body stocking beneath her spangled suit. She pushes a cart with several assault rifles on it.

The Concealment Artist asks Eddie to blindfold him. Eddie gets up and ties a heavy black cloth around the man's head. The artist says something about the weapons being specially licensed. The audience titters. The woman pushes a plastic stopwatch on stage. It is a meter in diameter and has the name of a Japanese manufacturer imprinted on its base. She calls go and starts the clock.

The artist's hands dazzle as they disassemble and reassemble the rifles. In thirty seconds he is finished with one; by the time two minutes are up, he has done all five. He strips off the blindfold and bows. The blindfold unfurls to become a cape. He drapes the cape over his arm and thrusts a rifle into it.

The artist waves the cape; the rifle is gone. He quickly

dispatches the other rifles as the crowd cheers. The house lights come up. The Concealment Artist bows and leaves the stage. Applause.

Eddie sits at the card table. The audience gives the artist a standing ovation. People chant MORE, MORE, MORE. The artist trots onstage, the cape around his neck.

He gestures broadly at Eddie. —I have forgotten my poor volunteer. He walks to the card table. —I'll make it up to you. What is your name?

—Eddie Niijls.

—Interesting. Russian? Perhaps Finnish?

—I'm not sure. Irish, I heard, from when the Danes were there. Maybe it's not true.

—They deigned name you? The artist winks to the crowd. —Eddie, you've been a great help, and in return, I'll tell your fortune.

He takes Eddie's hand. —I find this method best. That is, without splitting entrails. He squints at Eddie's palm. —Hmmm. Troubling. Perhaps you have used some solvent? The lines are indistinct. Are you, by chance, under a physician's care? No? Maybe you should be.

The crowd laughs.

—Oh, the artist says, I'm sure it's quite harmless. Suppose we try a more oracular approach. What to use? My sticks are at home, and I never carry coins during a performance.

He reaches into Eddie's shirt pocket. —Ah, what's this?

He pulls out a handful of cartridges. Eddie stares at them. They are as big as his fingers, long brass cases with copper-jacketed bullets ending in sharp tips of exposed lead. The artist swings the cartridges overhead, lets them go. They fall in a pattern on the card table.

—Khan, the artist says.

Eddie opens his mouth.

The artist puts up his hand. —A cave within a cave.

The lights go down.

—Evil despite sincerity.

Eddie looks at his shoes.

—Some deliverance. No error. Filling with water, but this line shows you have yet to go under. Some hope. Twice or thrice bound in the thickets of thorns. You find no way. There will be great evil.

Applause. Lights up. The artist exits. Eddie sits at the table, his head in his hands, as people leave the auditorium.

I V

Eddie takes the bus home. He sees the flashing lights of fire trucks and police cars.

The barrier an official line of yellow plastic. Security men in uniforms.

—Can I get in?

—Why?

—I live here.

—Which is yours?

—One-O-three.

—You're lucky. It was across the hall. How well do you know your neighbor?

—Not at all.

—You don't know anything, right? You never notice people coming and going, or what the neighbor does, or what model car he drives, or his license number, right?

—Sorry.

—Look, man, this is a community. Join up.

—When can I get in?

—There's an investigation in progress. You don't have any oily rags, do you? Leave your name and address.

—But where will I stay?

—Your problem. Don't make us come looking for you.

The man at the desk is friendly. His rich accent puts Eddie at ease. There is free cable.

It is colder. Winter coming on early maybe. Cold snap,

Eddie thinks. He will say that next time he talks to somebody. "Cold snap, huh?" Or, "Front moved down from Canada."

The line at the building gets longer and longer. The building's windows are covered, and the burnt-out doorway is sealed with steel mesh. The guards have a hut-like sentry box. They talk to people through a sliding window.

He thinks of the motel manager as Mr. Haji. Once a week, Mr. Haji asks about money. Eddie looks at the floor and says he has been promised a voucher.

The food does not come by voucher. An old woman shows Eddie where to get it. He meets her in line.

They give him a set amount. Mostly in cans. Cereals are his favorite. Oatmeal and white flour and corn meal. He works every day. With limited success, it is true. Bad materials are at fault: he glues the cereals to a piece of cardboard with toothpaste to simulate the cool tones of a suburban townhouse.

One day they give him a coat. A big stormcoat with frayed cuffs and lambswool lining and wide lapels. Old, but serviceable and warm.

Eddie has a plan. When the voucher comes through and he is able to pay Mr. Haji, he will need his own place. A base of operations.

He dreams now vividly. Of a woman. Dolores. And not Dolores. The dreams are passionate, varied, erotic.

Mr. Haji lends him a lint brush. The sky is threatening. Eddie carefully brushes the stormcoat inside and out. Tomorrow might be warm. He wishes he had a necktie. The pants and shirt they gave him are okay, but a tie would be nice.

He will get land. Not much. Anywhere. An acre of woods or part of a field. Dig a well. Outhouse, no plumbing.

Do without electricity. Maybe go south, save on heat. He could build it. From plywood. From tarpaper.

The first snowfall. Large, delicate flakes melt in Eddie's hair. He walks past the silent machine shops and warehouses and factories. Eddie enters a neighborhood of small houses with dirty, warped façades. Junkers line the streets and block driveways. Chained dogs bark.

He crosses the division street, a broad avenue. Eddie remembers his building. The one before. The artists' co-op. That building is far. Eddie grows tired.

Sometimes he forgets. He must get money from George.

An area of shops. Neat storefronts with colorful displays. Eddie looks for patterns. Navaho designs are big. He straightens the lapels of his stormcoat. He would like a hat, felt, with an inch-and-a-half brim, but he does not see any. They could be out. Some neckties with Van Goghs and Gauguins on them. Imports from Guatemala.

Eddie looks for George's Mercedes. Some of the stores look a little shabby. Cracked bricks; some mortar worn away. A gutted shop. Others burned out. Smashed windows. Posters advising citizens to turn in arsonists.

George's gallery is empty. Bands of masking tape form $X$'s on the windows. A sign gives a new address.

He could get there, maybe, by bus. Two transfers or three. It is a development. An old brewery. Shops and restaurants. Café tables with Cinzano umbrellas in the center court. He could sit at a table. First stop by the tobacco shop for Balkan Sobranies, then a pint of Irish lager and a snack, say calamari. Someone might stop. Friends of George, people he used to know. Maybe Dolores. She would not. Odds a million to one against. Have a look at the stores. Buy a new suit. Call her. Tell her to come by. Have a drink. She could laugh and be happy.

—You lost? Uniform. Riot stick.

—No.

—I think so. You wouldn't stand here otherwise.

—Thank you, I'm going. Thank you.

He is not sure when school gets out, but it is wise to detour around a few neighborhoods. The snow is heavier.

Eddie's feet are numb; the brogans they gave him soaked through. He is not sure where he is. He sees the printer's house. Eddie stumbles up the steps and tries to open the storm door, but his hands cannot work the handle. He keeps trying. His hands flop on the door like dying fish.

—My old customer. How can I help?

Eddie shakes. A press clacks as it prints out invitations. The printer pushes Eddie into a chair and brings him coffee.

—As you can see, I'm working today. Money coming in.

The house does not have to be much. The snow has slowed. He has a map the printer made for him. Eddie finds his way to his old neighborhood. If he can get land, the slab will be easy. It is getting dark as he nears his building. Framing he can do, and maybe use prefab joists. The ground vibrates. Sounds like metal tearing. Get a small wood stove, the basic model. There is a string of lights above the street. Some spotlights up ahead. The walls could be canvas. Old paintings. Staple them to both sides of the studs and stuff rags between them for insulation. Bulldozers push mounds of debris. Eddie's building is gone.

v

Eddie cannot go out. Sometimes someone comes to his door and knocks gently. Eddie stays in bed with the pillow over his face.

—Mr. Niijls, are you all right?

Eddie is tired and confused. He opens the door.

—You are ill? Mr. Haji says.

—No, no. I'm fine.

—I have disturbed you?

—No. No. Fine.

—Have you eaten?

—Yes. Fine. Fine. Eddie points to an empty soup can.

—I have bad news. You must leave tomorrow.

—The voucher—

—I am sorry.

Eddie goes to the bus stop. Most of his work was destroyed. But George must have some of it. Eddie has his work-in-progress in the suitcase Mr. Haji gave him. That could give him an entry—credibility.

The building is not as he envisioned it. The shops sell women's clothing or overpriced novelties. The restaurants sell French-inspired fast food. There is a lot of wrought iron and plastic ivy.

A drink, perhaps, to bolster him.

There are not any bars.

The art at George's strikes him strange. Wildlife and Indians and textured neutral hangings. People on horses.

—What is it? George says. He wears a dark suit with a wide chalk stripe. British-looking.

—You remember me?

—No. Eddie? The stone rolled away and Eddie returned? Extraordinary. Come.

He leads Eddie to an office. Blond desk, couch and matching chairs, patterned carpet.

—Everyone thought you were gone. There was some talk of California, I believe.

—I lost my place.

—Really? George sits down on the desk.

—Then I had to leave.

George nods. —Well, what is it? The help? Cash? Will that

settle us up? A job? Sorry, we're fully staffed. Take some of your work? Look at me, Eddie.

—I'm working on this thing, Eddie says. It's rough.

George sucks in his cheeks.

—I went to see the Concealment Artist.

—Shit, George says. What's an auto in the sock?

Eddie looks at the watch hanging from George's vest.

—Concentrate, Eddie.

George does not look like George. Same suit, but the man is radiant. Gentle. Warm.

EDDIE: Who're you?

B.O.S.: A businessman. Perhaps a bit more. You might say I'm something of a symbol to many people.

EDDIE: The Businessman of the Saved.

B.O.S.: Yes.

EDDIE: And you have a message?

B.O.S.: You came to me.

EDDIE: The message that will transform the world.

B.O.S. (*Laughing*): We must take the world as we find it.

EDDIE: Yes.

B.O.S.: This is not to say we desire stagnation.

EDDIE: The world as it is, only transformed.

B.O.S.: You're close, but while change is the only constant in the global marketplace, complete transformation is an abstraction. We're looking at reorganization in some localities and an inherent stagnation in others. Patterns of commercial transfer. Labor as a commodity. A movable base that allows for flexibility as resource and labor components are exhausted.

EDDIE: Exhausted?

B.O.S.: Have to run. Put together a package. Come along. Listen. Learn.

The Businessman of the Saved leads Eddie through corridors lined with offices and abstract paintings. They attend meetings. At length they reach the limousine. A chauffeur in a natty black uniform holds the door for them.

The car is like the loss of a half-remembered love as one wakes from dreaming.

EDDIE: Foreign job?

B.O.S.: Multinational. Body, engine, drivetrain—Japanese. American interior. Check the dash.

Eddie looks. Rich light shines through concentric crystalline spheres. The spheres rotate, emitting eerie, beautiful music. Small lights flicker. Devices as complex and delicate as gyroscopes spin to the music's rhythm.

EDDIE: Amazing. Where?

B.O.S.: Switzerland. Watch business isn't what it used to be, but the market sees no talent is wasted.

The condo is at the top of the tallest building in the world. They ride up in a glass express elevator. The chauffeur, Fritz, stands at attention near the control panel.

One wall of the condo is glass: it overlooks the downtown. The carpet is white, the furniture contemporary. Fritz comes out in a butler's uniform with a tray of cocktails.

The Businessman of the Saved motions Eddie to a chair. Fritz brings cigars. Eddie selects one. Fritz lights it with a silver lighter. The Businessman of the Saved picks up the remote control for the wide-screen high-definition TV.

B.O.S.: All this could be yours.

Eddie reclines, sinks into the warm leather. The Businessman of the Saved flips on the TV. Football. Eddie finishes his drink. Fritz removes the empty glass. The Businessman of the Saved nods. Fritz brings dry beer in crystal steins.

B.O.S.: There's the game, eh?

Eddie's mouth is full of dry beer. He nods.

B.O.S.: Spin the wheel.

He hits the remote. A video comes on. The dancing woman has long, tightly-curled hair.

B.O.S.: Behind the curtain.

Eddie is entranced by the dancer.

B.O.S.: Look, you deserve better.

Other videos. Fritz brings more beer and some snacks: chicken wings, herring, crudités, sushi, pickled okra, caviar, shrimp, escargots, oysters.

B.O.S.: Lost or stolen.

The game comes on again.

B.O.S.: Security. Look to the future.

Eddie's cigar has gone out. He turns his head to the side and closes his eyes.

B.O.S.: Over fifty years' experience.

Eddie hears music, but he cannot open his eyes.

B.O.S.: Clink of fine crystal.

Someone running for a touchdown, the announcer's voice rising, the roar of the crowd.

B.O.S.: The envy of the world.


Eddie wakes. Fritz is carrying him toward a microvan. He has been wrapped in a blanket.

—What happened?

—You had a little spell.

The van drops Eddie downtown.


V I

Eddie suffers misfortune. Three men with a butcher knife rob him. He has two dollars. He gives them the money and his digital watch and tells them that is it. They take his shoes. There is snow on the ground. Eddie steals clothes from a laundromat dryer and wraps his feet. He begs enough for a small hamburger and coffee and keeps on, following the freeway towards the printer's house.

Eddie avoids people.


The printer is on the porch. Two bulbs burn in the ceiling fixture. Eddie pounds on the door.

—Are you all right? The printer looks at Eddie's feet.

—Yeah. The rags are soaked with blood. Eddie looks out

at the pink footprints, the history of his progress, in the snow.
—I'll be fine.

—Uh huh. What is it this time?

The floor is covered with parts—metal type, heavy levers, intricate gears and toothed flywheels, frames. Dead-looking steel or cast iron.

—I see you're busy.

The printer bends over a table, adjusts a goose-necked lamp, picks up an Allen wrench. He squints, frowns, steps back. The wrench hangs loosely in his hand.

—Maybe you could spare me a minute? Eddie says.

The printer crosses the room, takes a monocle from the desk, claps it on his eye. —You're back. Tell me something that wasn't inevitable. He smiles weakly, his large eyes watery and gentle. —Have some coffee. He motions toward the percolator.

—MISTER COME BACK NOW, the printer says. MISTER I ONLY VISIT WHEN I'M IN TROUBLE BECAUSE I DON'T WANT MY FANCY FRIENDS TO SEE.

The printer's hand sweeps over the destroyed presses. —All in pieces and you're all of a piece. And you like a son to me.

EDDIE: The Businessman of the Damned.

B.O.D.: Your useless education was purchased with toil and sweat. Never forget that.

EDDIE: Have I?

B.O.D.: Have I told you never to forget that?

EDDIE: The press?

B.O.D.: Not beyond repair. New models cost a fortune.

EDDIE: All those pieces.

B.O.D.: Got to fix her. That baby's got to last another season at least.

EDDIE: Scrimp . . . long-range . . . capital investment.

B.O.D.: Don't spout theory; we've work to do. Look at this

place. Nobody gave me a handout, mister, nor a leg up, nor a bloody fucking bootstrap to pull. Uh, no offense.

EDDIE: Huh?

B.O.D.: I'd always dreamed you would return, and the old woman dreamed so as well, God rest her soul. Gave us comfort on many a cold night.

EDDIE: What?

B.O.D. (*A tear rolls down his cheek*): It's true all this doesn't look like much compared to life in the army, I mean in the city, I mean in those beer commercials.

EDDIE: It's cold in here.

B.O.D. (*Tenderly*): And a cold coming you had of it. Take some of those lousy rags from your feet and stuff 'em in the window there. That'll cut the wind at least.

Eddie does as he is told.

B.O.D.: Still and all, we'll get her into shape. When she's a going concern, you'll feel like a new man. (*He takes up a rasp*) Many of the parts are usable yet, and those that aren't we'll machine ourselves.

EDDIE: I don't know.

B.O.D.: Don't expect you to. You're only an apprentice.

EDDIE: A printer's devil?

B.O.D.: You'll be expected to demonstrate your loyalty to the firm. No wages. But maybe we can find you some socks, eh? (*B.O.D. laughs heartily*) No, just joshing you. You'll have your socks, and boots as well. You'll have your keep.

EDDIE: Um.

B.O.D.: You're home.

Eddie's feet heal in the boots. There is never enough light for the work. The food is monotonous: oatmeal, black bread, beans, rice. The stray chunk of stringy meat. Weak coffee. Tap water. They work twelve hours a day. There is no clock in the shop. Eddie sleeps on a mat in the corner, his stormcoat for a blanket.

He studies the Businessman of the Damned's visage. The

sickly pallor. Thin hair. Rotten teeth. Bloodshot eyes. There are no mirrors in the shop.

The door bursts open. Fritz in an iridescent black uniform, a long stiletto in hand. He glances around, raises the shades, closes the knife and puts it in his jacket. The Businessman of the Saved enters.

B.O.D.: A great honor.

B.O.S.: Greetings. *(He sees Eddie)* How could you cross alive into this gloom?

EDDIE: Hello.

B.O.D.: Don't mind him, he's learning the trade.

B.O.S.: Ah, the trade.

B.O.D.: To carry on when I'm gone.

B.O.S.: Just so. Fritz!

Fritz opens a briefcase and shows its contents to the Businessman of the Damned. Eddie moves over to the type cabinet. Fritz and the Businessman of the Damned converse. The Businessman of the Saved sidles up to Eddie.

B.O.S.: Part of the family tradition?

EDDIE: Well . . .

B.O.S.: I should have brought milk. Meat. Blood. What have you been feeding on?

EDDIE: Oh.

B.O.S.: Destined to grinding labors like my own in the sunny world?

EDDIE: I had to go somewhere.

B.O.S.: Not so bad a hole as many one could fall into. But what future?

EDDIE: It's temporary.

B.O.S.: Without saying. Communications, what better? But these relics? In the satellite era?

EDDIE: What else is there?

FRITZ: All finished here, sir.

B.O.S.: Good.

The Businessman of the Saved claps the Businessman of

the Damned on the back, shakes his hand, slips him a fifty-dollar bill.

FRITZ *(To Eddie)*: Better . . . sod . . . iron rations . . . Lord, it . . . exhausted dead.

B.O.S. *(To Eddie in stage whisper)*: You're surprised? The old bastard's the father of us all.

B.O.D.: Thank you. This is a day we'll long remember. A visit by a personage of Your Eminence's stature. And the work. We're not down to our last crust, but close enough, sir, close enough. Good for the lad as well, to see the caliber of people a businessman encounters. Puts me in mind of the boy's dear mother . . .

EDDIE *(A tear rolls down his cheek)*: My mother . . .

B.O.D.: I'm not alone, sir, in feeling it would be an appropriate memorial to yourself and your outstanding service to the community.

B.O.S.: There was some talk of an equestrian statue. But it's not about recognition.

B.O.D.: Indeed.

B.O.S.: It's about love.

B.O.D.: Hark you, lad. Work and love.

B.O.S.: Love and work.

FRITZ *(A tear rolls down his cheek)*: It is not possible to live without love.

Fritz and the Businessman of the Saved go out the door and down the steps.

EDDIE: . . . yes I will Yes.

### V I I

The truth falls on Eddie like the weight of the world. He must cross the city and go to Dolores. There is no room for weakness.

As the printer sleeps, Eddie rises from his mat. He thinks about leaving a note, but no language will soften the blow for the old man.

He takes a crowbar, compensation for his labors, and slips

out. A knife would be better, but the old man keeps the obvious weapons locked up. The crowbar serves. It is eighteen inches long and has a comfortable heft.

He will move at night, save the days for rest. Eddie will do what he has to do. Everything else is secondary. He checks parked cars for valuables.

A man carrying a heavy grocery bag. No one else on the street. Eddie moves towards the entryway of an apartment building.

—Yo. Hold up, the man says.

—What? Eddie says. Hand on the crowbar inside his coat.

—Hold up. The man limps toward him. —I'm hurt.

—Come closer, you'll be dead. Eddie brings out the crowbar. I'll fuck you up.

—Help me. The man holds up the bag. I'll share.

—Give me the bag, Eddie says.

—Help me or leave me; I keep the bag.

—I could kill you and take it.

The man looks at the ground.

Everything comes out of the bag: antiseptic, ointment, gauze, bandages. The wound is in the thigh, an ugly puncture, but whether it is a gun or a knife job, Eddie cannot say.

The man will not tell. —Just help. You'll get your reward.

—What if there's a projectile in the tissue?

—My problem.

—I'm no doctor—

—Then shut up.

Eddie cleans the wound, packs it, wraps it securely. He is careful not to cut off the circulation. —You'll be okay if there's no infection.

The man opens the sack. —What do you want?

—Got a car in there?

Bagman laughs. —Here. He hands Eddie a half-pint of whiskey.

—That's it?

—All right. He gives Eddie a joint.

—And?

—Here. He gives Eddie a russet potato.

Eddie lights the joint and opens the bottle. They smoke and drink in the doorway.

Bagman explains everything: Eddie's problem is that he does not have any money. Maybe Bagman will take Eddie in. Eddie is grateful and wary. They sleep bundled in rags in a refrigerator box beneath a railway trestle. Bagman keeps a small chrome-plated revolver to discourage the inhabitants of the neighboring hovels from coming by. Eddie has not forgotten Dolores.

Bagman's leg is almost healed. He tells Eddie to wait by the box while he goes spotting. Eddie waits all day. He bakes potatoes in the embers of a garbage fire.

Bagman returns at dusk. They eat.

—Let's go.

—Where?

—Watch. I'll show you what to do.

They walk for miles through blocks of concrete flats. It is dark when Bagman stops. He hops into a window well and pries the security bars from the window frame with a flat piece of steel. He makes a large X on the glass with masking tape, delivers a sharp rap with the steel. The glass breaks neatly. Most of it pulls out on the tape.

Eddie follows him through the window. Bagman holds the steel like a bludgeon, checks the rooms. A night light is on in the bathroom. Bagman ransacks the bureau. Eddie hesitates. Bagman points at the closet. Eddie sorts through the hanging clothes, the shoes on the floor. He does not see anything of value, just clothes, shoes.

Bagman fills his pockets and leads Eddie into the front room. They are disconnecting the speaker wires. The door is kicked in. Uniformed men. Shotgun pointed at Eddie. He grabs Bagman. Pulls. The gun goes off. Bagman in front of Eddie. Sagging.

Eddie unharmed. —Small shot, he says.

Bagman falls.

Eddie is in the window frame.

Out.

Running.

Eddie waits in the box. He is afraid he is covered with blood. There are tests which could link him to Bagman's death. He strips off his clothes. The smallest trace of organic material, a drop of blood, bit of tissue, a hair, is enough to hang him. Eddie cannot find a trace.

He remembers something about bloody footprints. Tracks. He checks his boots. No blood.

He waits and hopes.

Sirens and shouts wake him. The noise is meaningless. Then he knows they are after him. Bagman, if alive, ratted him. Eddie wriggles out of the box. Shots and screams. He runs with the neighbors from nearby boxes and hootches. They move toward the bottom of the gorge, hoping to get across and get lost on the opposite slope. The uniformed men follow in a line. Their pace is leisurely. They set shacks on fire, reload their automatic pistols and jam birdshot into their shotguns, joke. Everything is easy. A bugle sounds far off. Olive-drab helicopter twirls overhead. Eddie dives for the opposite slope.

The houses are large stone or brick or mock-Tudor structures with high walls around them. The streets are empty except for the occasional patrol car. Eddie stays close to the walls. The sun rises. Dolores lives on the East Side of the city. Eddie goes east.

A man in a cashmere coat walks a Doberman pinscher.
—Edward? It is George.

—Where am I? Eddie says.

—My neighborhood. This is my dog, King Louis Onze.
The Doberman growls.

—Now, now, George says.

Eddie puts his hand on the crowbar inside his coat.
—Look, George, I really need help.

—Now, there are limits.

—Please. I'll do anything you say.

—Walk with me; we'll talk.

The sun shines bright. Birds sing. A milk truck makes its
rounds through the clean, wide alleys.

—Maybe I can help. George takes a pipe from his pocket,
fills it from a leather pouch, lights it with a gold lighter. —First,
tell me what you've done wrong.

—Me? Nothing. Eddie's hand rests on the cool metal.

—Come now, George says, confess your crimes.

—I haven't done anything.

—What have you thought? Felt?

—Anxiety and despair.

—Hmmm, George says. I've seen this before.

—You know about it?

—All this suffering, Edward, all this hopelessness. There's
a way out.

—How? Tell me.

George stops. Louis Onze heels, sits, teeth bared.

—At the end of a rope. George laughs. Louis Onze throws
back his head and howls. George begins to cough and doubles
over. He thrusts out his hand. There is a business card between his fingers. —Take it. He coughs.

Eddie looks at the card. On one side a cartoon of a hanged
man. A phone number on the other.

—Call, George says. He coughs. His face turns blue. Eddie
steps behind him and pats him on the back. George sways.

Louis Onze springs at Eddie, misses. A van rounds the corner. Louis Onze springs again. Eddie swings the crowbar. Louis Onze catches the crowbar in his teeth and wrenches it from Eddie's hand. George falls down. The van stops. Men rush at Eddie. Louis Onze charges one of the men. The man draws a nine-millimeter pistol and fires. Louis Onze falls. George goes into convulsions. A man hits Eddie on the side of the face with a club. Eddie stumbles. A man points a pistol at him.

—Shit, another man says. He stabs Eddie in the abdomen with a long, thin-bladed knife. Eddie twists; half the blade breaks off inside him. He stumbles and jerks, circles in a little dance, runs.

Eddie in an alley. There is a small space, maybe four feet wide, bordered by a garage on one side and a stone wall on two others. Safe from sight. Exposed only to the back of a house. He climbs up on some trash cans, hoists himself to the top of the wall, falls face-down into the space. The snow cushions his fall. He sinks deep and sleeps a black, dreamless sleep.

Crisp snap of the breaking crust on the snow. Eddie's eyes open. He cannot focus. He blinks. A mucus covers his eyes.

—Hey. A child's voice.

—Hey, Dad.

Eddie opens his mouth. His jaw cracks. Sharp pain in the joint. Flapping tongue, numb lips. He gives off a harsh rasp.

The snap of an automatic pistol's slide. —I'll take care of this, Son.

—Don't, Eddie says. I'll go. When I catch my breath. He tries to sit up. —I'm hurt.

—You're on my property. Move or I'll kill you.

—Please. Let me stay. Until I heal. I'll watch the place.

—Impractical.

—Can we cut off his eyelids, Dad?

—Not now, Son.

—Please, Eddie says.

—Go get the manacles out of my toolbox.

Eddie's left wrist is chained to an iron ring in the wall. He sleeps. When he is not sleeping, he watches. There is milky light with shapes in it. He grows thin but keeps sinking through the snow and rotting leaves to the earth. Eddie feels himself unfleshed. His skeleton leaves a hard silver imprint on the ground, a permanent image that freezes and thaws will never eradicate. He knows where the knife is in him. The point is stuck in one of his ribs. Perhaps the blade will dissolve by spring and he will be free. No one disturbs his peace.

### VIII

Rain falls gently, then in long lines. Sheets. He does not sink. A wet dog howls. The rains slack off. A sunny day. A couple more. Grass and weeds come up. The mud dries. He sits. One day he stands. Walks. Until the chain stops him. He goes back to the wall. Out again. And back.

They lengthen the chain. Later take it off. Give him some cord and a plastic tarp. He rigs the tarp, attaching it to the stone wall and garage. He does not enter the house; it never occurs to him. The boy brings him things: cold coffee, a cigarette, bit of chocolate, half can of imported beer.

Sometimes in the cool of the evening, he walks with the man. Other times, he squats beneath his hootch and scratches strange glyphs in the dirt with a stick. The boy watches. He shows the boy things—perspective, vanishing point. The boy brings a pencil stub and paper.

The man mentions sketches. He found the boy in the boy's room, drawing. The man examined the pictures closely; any good parent would do the same. Frankly, the man was impressed with the quality of the work.

Perhaps some arrangement can be made. Say the man were to supply the artist materials, working space, and his keep. In the house. The artist could be a sort of temporary member of the family.

Of course, there are limits. The artist is a craftsman, no doubt, but this is not a commission to run riot. The family is primary, and everyone must know his place in it.

The artist is deloused, shaved, barbered. The man gives him an old suit. The artist finds a five-dollar bill in the vest pocket. The man leads the artist downstairs to a subbasement. Square room with crumbling limestone walls. Bare bulb. Metal cot, no mattress, wire net instead of springs. Wooden table. Scrap lumber stacked in the corner.

Studies are made. Standard practice. Cartoons. Not in the pejorative sense. Materials are in short supply. And time is valuable. Not that he is to rush. What is wanted is a quality product. Something to hang on to. Something that will increase in value. But it has to be in one take. For now, he will have snapshots to work from. Retrain his eye.

They pose in the living room. The man and boy stand. The woman sits between them in a Victorian easy chair.

The artist wants the boy in the foreground.

—We've made our decision, the man says.

—But—

—I believe we have a verbal contract. When you were hungry, as it were, you voiced no objections.

—It's just a suggestion.

—Very well. The man turns to his family. —There's a suggestion.

—Uh.

—Please proceed.

—The boy could go here. It would make balance.

—Balance is not the point.

—In a way it is.

—He'll obscure his mother. What sort of family history will this be with the boy's mother only half there?

—There's a precedent.

—Really?

—Traditional. The boy projecting into the future.

—Never heard of such a thing.

—You've seen it. The holy family.

—Holy family?

—Imagine.

—Yes, yes.

He gets their shapes. The man brings lights and paint to the artist's room. A photo of the family is blown up to poster size in case there is a problem. Brushes are supplied as needed, but the artist has only one canvas.

The artist roughs in the rows of flowers on the wallpaper. He puts in the chandelier and pedestal table, the bust of Caesar and the aquarium. He is doing the ceiling, spreading some flat white with a putty knife, when he tears the canvas.

The man is not happy. There are three tears now, above the family and on either side of them. The artist assures the man this happens all the time. What is needed is a bit of canvas so he can patch the tears. None of this will be visible to the untrained eye.

He plasters Chinese white over the torn areas and puts his work on the patches: birds and reptiles, the sun and moon in various relations, a dog howling at a ladder that reaches into the night sky. Before the paint has completely dried, he patches over the images with fresh canvas.

A man's face, a heart, a playing card. He blanks them out. Tigers, foreign gods, guns, gangsters of earlier eras, house plans, diamond-shaped convergences of lines with spheres at each intersection, precious stones. Dolores.

The artist awakes.

—If you're so goddamn fucking intelligent, the man says, so bloody fucking superior, why do you live in my storeroom?

The boy hops up and down. The woman weeps, her face covered.

The man turns towards the boy, inadvertently pointing the pistol at him. —For the love of God, settle down.

He points the pistol at the artist.

—Get out.

The artist pulls on his trousers.

The man racks the slide. —Now.

The artist puts his feet in his shoes and grabs his clothes. He glances at the painting.

—Move your ass.

The artist realizes he has no shirt. He puts on his vest and jacket and jams his tie in his pocket. He buys a pack of cigarettes and a beer at a minimart. Two pay phones are mounted on the outer wall of the store. He steps to the nearest phone. The receiver is missing, the silver cord cut.

I X

The sergeant buzzes Eddie in. He limps, feet blistered, half-starved, over the threshold.

—Number? the sergeant says.

Eddie blinks.

—Give me the number, the sergeant says. The one you called.

Eddie stammers out the number.

The sergeant shakes his head. —Pathetic.

Another room: examining table, scale, desk, sink,

shiny wastebasket. A man in a labcoat comes in. —You're a relative?

—Uh, Eddie says.

—Here for a checkup? Company physical?

—They said wait. He gives the man a form.

—You? The man takes Eddie's pulse. Feels his biceps. —You must have some kind of connection to get you across.

—Well—

—Don't tell me; somebody made a call. He thumps Eddie's chest, listens to Eddie's heart. —It's pumping. I can certify that.

—That's—

—That's enough, huh? He hits Eddie's knee with a hammer. —Mostly we don't bother with this anymore. He pulls back Eddie's eyelid. —In your case, I think a conservative approach appropriate. The man sits down at the desk. —I'm going to ask you a few questions.

They wrap cuffs around his arms and ankles, belt him to a chair, put a metal cap on his shaved head, place suction-cuplike monitors over his nipples, eyelids, kidneys, testicles.

The leader is an older man. He tells the younger ones to shut up, goes to a wall-mounted panel, pushes some buttons. Eddie's chair slides into a rounded plastic tunnel. The tunnel fills with blue light.

The leader speaks. —Note the clarity of the image, and this without injection.

The light is constant. Eddie hears buzzing. He wishes it would stop.

—Unnecessary in a healthy individual. Notice the lesion in the lower quadrant. Hideous, yes, but we have an obligation.

The chair vibrates. In tune with the buzz. He is shaking.

—Atoms.

—And the bone mass, disturbing. This degree of deterioration is extraordinary.

Eddie's teeth chatter.

—See to that.

The light goes white and the buzzing stops. One of the younger ones jams a piece of plastic between Eddie's teeth.

—Clear.

The hum and blue light return.

—Besides, it would take half an hour to sew the son of a bitch back on. Necrosis and near-total occlusion. Let's in for a closer look.

The light turns violet. Eddie sweats.

—Laser treatment.

—Prolonged therapy options?

—Complications?

The soles of his feet are burning. He tries to scream, but the mouthpiece gags him.

—Particles of light, yes.

Smell of burning flesh.

—Bloody shame we haven't a dissection clearance. Wind it down.

Eddie hangs limp in the restraints. He cannot get the air into his lungs.

A fast open hand to the face startles him. Eddie opens his eyes, jerks back in his chair.

The leader tosses a form onto his lap. —Don't bother to thank me.

They give him an orange jumpsuit and canvas slippers. He is blindfolded and forced onto a bench. The room moves. He realizes he is in a truck.

—Hit it running, the sergeant says.

Eddie runs. The man beside him slows. A sergeant catches the man across the kidneys with a rubber truncheon.

They run everywhere. Eddie never asks questions. They clean the barracks, the yards, the roadways, the mess. Run, clean, exercise. There is a sign over the gate. No one knows what it says. A few of the others disappear. Then more. Eddie notices the empty bunks. He does not ask.

. . .

The sergeants refer to them as trainees. They are allowed to play basketball on Sunday mornings. The calisthenics give way to basic martial postures.

They go to a lecture hall. A man talks. He has a wooden pointer and a tripod for displays. The lectures have titles.

—In the classroom, the sergeant says, it's theory.

They stand in ranks on the drill field. Five men have been chosen. Eddie is lucky; he is still in the ranks. The sergeant arms four of the men with truncheons, etches a square in the dirt, posts an armed man at each corner. The unarmed man is placed inside the square.

—Survival, the sergeant says. He steps out of the square.

Eddie's legs twitch. He knows not to lock his knees. It is hot. He is thirsty.

—Often seen, the sergeant says, as dichotomy. Us and them, he and she, I and thou. Presumes all oppositions are merely bipolar.

The sergeant lights a cigarette. —Reality is a bit more complicated. This is baby play.

The exercise begins.

A sergeant pulls him from his rack. Eddie wakes in midair, hits the concrete floor, tries to get up.

—Stay there.

Eddie hears the boots on the floor and knows they are forming a circle.

—Struggle, the sergeant says.

Eddie covers his face.

They go on and on. The sergeant screams. The others kick, shout accusations. The sergeant hits Eddie with a garbage-can lid.

Eddie remembers.

—I confess, he says.

—He confesses, the sergeant says.

The sergeant pulls Eddie up and drags him across the barracks to the reeducation cell. He punches Eddie in the stomach.

—Examine your conscience, motherfucker.


No one is to blame. Eddie has accused others. He is happy to be back with the group.

He releases the safety on his weapon before the command has been given. Eddie is in the prone position. Everyone hears the click. The range sergeant kicks him in the small of the back. Eddie makes no sound.

When the others are dismissed, the sergeant calls him over to the office.

—You all right?

—I confess, Eddie says, I confess.

—Relax. It takes time. You'd be surprised how many of us started as something else.

—Really?

—Why, I was a psychologist, the sergeant says. Imagine it.


Although he is clumsy and slow and not the best shot, Eddie is named Most Improved Trainee and given a special honor. A dignitary is to be laid in state at Headquarters, and Eddie will serve on the honor guard. A sergeant brings him to the empty rotunda and walks him through the routine at midnight. The sound of their steps echoes through the dome.

Two medical officers wheel a casket in.

—Pop it, the sergeant says.

—Not a good idea.

—We have to be sure he's there, the sergeant says.

The doc opens the coffin. They crowd in for a look. The face has been pumped up with fluid and rouged.

—Holy shit, Eddie says. His knees lock.

—Get a hold of yourself.

—Is it? Eddie says.

—We salute the uniform, the sergeant says, not the man.

X

—There's been some talk of winding down, the group leader says. Let me tell you, we are not winding down. Economics is war by other means. We welcome this new era, this restructuring.

They huddle, lock their hands atop each others', chant *Go, go, go,* push down, and break. They run past the weapons lockers, up the ramp, into the vans.

Eddie hangs on to a metal ring in the van's wall.

—Today, Jim says, a small raid.

—Small? Eddie says.

—Yeah, minimal mortality. Shouldn't be any resistance. If we take heavy fire, work your way back to the truck. Somebody'll be along for us.

A sergeant crawls back from the cab. —We're gonna hit a business. Shake 'em up.

—Who is it? somebody says.

—Some old bastard who wants to hang on. Not bad, just useless.

Eddie follows Jim out of the van. It is dark, and someone is shooting out the streetlights.

Eddie winces. —What?

—Helps the mystique, Jim says.

They move toward a house. There is a sign out front. Two men beat it with sledge hammers. The point men smash in the door with a battering ram. A figure runs from the back of the house. No one goes after him. He crosses the street and disappears into some low buildings.

They go inside the house. Broken machinery and smashed furniture. Men throw paper, dishes, clothes. Jim hands Eddie a can of spray paint.

—Do the walls.

—What do you want on them?

—Be creative.

Jim shoots a cat. —Always kill the pets, it's our trademark.

Eddie paints a sunburst and the words DO NOT RETURN. He is doing EXAMINE YOUR CONSCIENCE when he hears shouts.

There is a billboard on the roof of a two-story building across the street. The printer stands on the billboard's catwalk. Eddie draws his pistol.

—Don't. Jim forces Eddie's arm down. —Light him up.

Somebody fires a flare. Eddie is entranced by the sharp trajectory of the rise, the pop of the tiny parachute, the swaying fall and carnival-like light.

—Don't be discouraged, the printer shouts.

—Idiot, Jim says.

Men carry jerrycans from the vans to the house.

—Allow for expansion, the printer says. No problems, only opportunities.

—Fire it.

—Ready on red.

—We can compete with anybody, the printer says.

—Fire in the hole.

The house explodes.

They go to restaurants and pick up envelopes, or to movies or bars or stores. The shopkeepers are accommodating; they offer Eddie and Jim gifts. Jim introduces Eddie to a tailor who alters their uniforms. Eddie starts wearing shiny, nonregulation sunglasses like Jim's.

On a pleasant evening, they work foot patrol by the river. It is dusk, and the woods on the river's banks give the air a fresh smell.

Eddie listens to the birds in the trees, lights an imported cigar. —This is why we trained so hard, eh, Jim?

—Yeah. Jim scans the area. He motions towards the expensive houses across the road. —This is nice, but always watch the woods.

—Yeah?

—Bad people. A lot of bad people down there.

A man and a woman walk the trail beside the houses. Eddie

notices their hiking shoes and colorful outfits. They are young and clean and fit. Productive people. People worth defending.

—What we ought to do, Jim says, is sweep the fuckers out.

—Yeah.

—Burn the woods. Get their fucking nest.

They walk a winding dirt road that descends to a park at the water's edge. A sign says the park closes at sundown. The gravel lot is almost empty. Rusted-out van parked near the cedar-shingled pavilion. Across the lot, a new model Japanese sedan. The hood is up and two kids lean over the engine.

—I don't like it, Jim says. Look at their shoes.

One wears scuffed boots. The other, ripped canvas sneakers. Eddie unsnaps his holster.

—Step back from the car, Jim shouts.

The kids jerk. One's arm goes back. Eddie draws his pistol. A tire iron flies, clatters short on the gravel. Jim fires. The one who threw the iron falls; the other runs. Eddie tries to get him in the sights. Jim fires. The second kid falls. Jim picks up the tire iron.

They move to the car. The battery is disconnected. The first kid is dead, chest cavity hit. The other whimpers.

—You throw things at me? Jim says.

—Let me go.

—You assault me, and I should forget it? What happened to the owner?

—Nothing.

—Then where the fuck is he?

—We never saw him.

Jim smiles at Eddie. —The owner's an invisible man. Then they attack us.

—Please, the kid says.

Jim hits him with the tire iron. —Shut up.

The kid breathes hard.

—Maybe we should give him a break, Eddie says.

—Who the fuck ever gave us a break?

They dump the bodies in the river.

· · ·

Jim drives. They circle a shopping mall. Once, twice, three or four times.

—Nothing here, Eddie says.

—Yeah, Jim says. He goes up the service road to the freeway ramp. —Man, this job.

—Yeah, Eddie says.

Jim enters the freeway and zips across three lanes. Eddie looks at the speedometer. They are forty over the limit.

—It's like rolling a rock up a hill, Jim says. The car moves faster, dodges a pickup, a cab, a truck full of oxygen tanks.

—Should we use the siren? Eddie says.

—You get to the top, fucker rolls back down. Know what I mean?

A light rain begins to fall. They are going a hundred and fifteen. Eddie sits straight up in his seat, feet braced against the floor.

—Like that thing at the river.

—Yeah, Eddie says.

—I know you're new, Jim says, so I don't want to say anything.

—Say what? Go ahead.

—I'll say this, Jim says, and we'll just leave it there. Right? Eddie nods.

Jim blasts by a minivan and passes a poultry truck by swerving onto the shoulder. Rocks fly.

—Don't ever go soft on me again.

Eddie realizes his mistake and works to improve. He spends time at the gym working on the killing mind.

He thinks he is alone, turns and sees Jim standing on the sidelines.

—You need me? Eddie says.

—Just stopped by. You're coming along.

—Thanks.

—Let's go for a drink.

Eddie follows Jim outside. The evening is unseasonably crisp. A few faint stars are visible.

—You know about the Lost Kings? Jim says.

—No.

Jim lights a cigarette and hands Eddie the pack. —Once met an old man who'd known them. People claim they were called Kings 'cause they were the best, but that's bullshit. There were two brothers named King, and the rest got tagged that, too.

—They were aggressive. May have been five; they invented the five-man point system. They worked nights. Back then there was no real support. Maybe one helicopter for the whole city.

—One night, there was rioting. Flying columns of looters: hit here, then gone. In those warrens they had for projects. The Kings went in, kept radio contact, were mopping up. They were supposed to wait for trucks to pick 'em up in the morning. The city wasn't so built up; there was just a field on the outskirts. They got there and called.

—The trucks go out. Half an hour between the call and the field. No Kings. They wait awhile, call more people. Not a trace. They go street to street, building to building, room to room. Bring in dynamite and wrecking balls. Field gets bigger and bigger, but they don't find anything. For a long time after, they tested every piece of bone that washed down a gulley, but the Kings never turned up.

—Where's the field? Eddie says.

—Put it at every point on the compass. Somebody's built over it by now.

Eddie decorates the inside of his locker with pictures of women. They all look like a woman Eddie knew years ago named Dolores. When the locker is covered, he puts more pictures on the inner lid of his footlocker. Sometimes he allows himself to believe one of the women is Dolores. But only for a moment. Not always the same picture; that would be odd. It is nothing. A momentary diversion. A release.

The other men have similar quirks. The men believe in luck. They carry charms: religious medals, bracelets, watches, special holsters, knives, lanyards, flashlights. Some have tattoos which are said to protect them. Jim carries a folded playing card in his wallet; no one is allowed to see its face.

Things get collected. Jim checks suspects for valuables and weapons. He keeps what he wants and throws the rest down a sewer. Jim has stuff in a rented garage across town, but that is the accumulation of years' work. The others have strongboxes or sacks in their footlockers. They bring in rings, necklaces, gold teeth, earrings.

In the beginning, Eddie is squeamish. He feels something about taking a ring from a corpse's finger. He builds a small collection.

There are riots in the Spring. Eddie is surprised by the hostility. When he and Jim take ordinary suspects, the suspects speak softly. They do not dare be noticed. The mobs are filled with hatred. Eddie knocks one down, and the guy keeps trying to fight while Eddie and some others beat him. The guy cannot hurt them; anyone with sense would roll up, cover himself. Why claw air? Sometimes Eddie and the others throw money into the crowds. Then, when they are really going good, Jim lights them up with a flamethrower.

The sector is pacified. Eddie is too tired to take off his body armor. He hits his rack and sleeps for three days.

—Hurry up, you're late, Jim says.

—What?

—There's a lecture. Jim pulls Eddie from the bunk.

—Okay. Eddie starts to unbuckle his vest.

—No time.

Jim leads Eddie through a side door. The men sit cross-legged in ranks on the polished wooden floor. The speaker is behind a bulletproof glass shield. Eddie recognizes the shining countenance. The speaker dismisses the audience. Men filter out. The speaker walks towards Eddie. A chauffeur follows closely behind.

—We're in for it, Jim says.

—Hello, the Businessman of the Saved says.

Eddie cannot focus his eyes. —Old problem.

Fritz bows. —Hi ya.

EDDIE: You've lost some weight?

B.O.S.: No.

EDDIE: New suit perhaps?

B.O.S.: Afraid not.

EDDIE: Tinted contacts?

B.O.S.: Naw.

EDDIE: Colored your hair?

B.O.S.: No, no, no, no.

Fritz' hand goes inside his coat.

B.O.S.: Easy. He's a friend.

EDDIE: Really?

B.O.S.: Of sorts.

Fritz salutes. Jim straightens up and salutes.

B.O.S. (Waving them away): Dismissed.

Jim marches quickly out. Fritz follows.

B.O.S.: Adjusting?

EDDIE: I guess.

B.O.S.: Old Faustian bargain, what?

EDDIE: I don't know.

B.O.S.: You will.

The Businessman of the Saved walks Eddie out of the building. Fritz waits by a sleek, severely-angled helicopter.

B.O.S.: You want to go up in the bird?

EDDIE: Really?

FRITZ: The schedule?

B.O.S.: Come along; we'll up for a quick look.

They strap themselves into the plush seats. Fritz closes the hatch and takes the controls. The lift-off is smooth, like the ascent of a powerful elevator. Eddie closes his eyes.

B.O.S.: Feeling all right?

Eddie moans.

B.O.S.: Get a grip, man.

EDDIE: Yuh.

B.O.S.: Hey, open up. Take a look out there.

Eddie looks. The city is a series of concentric rings. Smoke rises from a few ruins, but the office complexes and freeways shine in the sun, and Eddie is struck, mostly, by the beauty.

B.O.S.: Now, you see our launching pad?

EDDIE: It's different from up here.

B.O.S.: There. In the center. Prime location, no? I know what you're thinking: what about expansion? Could yesterday's prime location be dead weight today?

EDDIE: Is it possible?

The helicopter flies gracefully toward the fields and wooded hills beyond the city. Eddie looks at the new suburbs, as perfect as architects' models.

B.O.S.: Air's nicer, eh?

The rotor stops spinning.

FRITZ: Aowaowowow.

B.O.S.: Goddamnit, he has these' spells.

The aircraft lists to one side.

B.O.S.: Fritz!

The helicopter loses altitude. Some houses clustered around a pond. A field beyond. The Businessman of the Saved grabs a parachute and begins strapping it on.

B.O.S.: Everything's fine. Fine, fine.

EDDIE: We're all going to die.

Eddie knows the field. He stands up. The copter circles.

EDDIE: That's it.

The copter drops gently.

EDDIE: The Field of Lost Kings.

B.O.S.: Lore of the trade.

EDDIE *(He shoulders Fritz aside, grabs the controls)*: We're going in.

B.O.S.: No such place. Let go.

Eddie wakes. His mouth and eyes are stuck shut. He licks his lips. Blood. —Am I dead and in hell, then?

The wreckage of the copter is a few hundred yards away in a grove of charred oak. Someone has wrapped Eddie in a parachute. He lies quietly in the silken cocoon until Jim and some others come along and load him into an ambulance. After a few days in the infirmary, he is sent back to the barracks and kept under observation.

Eddie wants to get back to work.

The cutbacks come. Men are assembled on the parade ground.

—Sorry, lads, the chief says, I held off as long as I could. It's politics, same as always, fucking politics.

Eddie is a member of the horde that snakes through a maze of tables and desks, returning issued equipment. He had not realized there were so many. He is given a cheap suit and his pay, and he manages to smuggle out a coffee can full of jewelry and other loot.

Eddie passes through the front gate. Fritz and the Businessman of the Saved stand by a refrigerated truck, handing out frozen turkeys.

B.O.S.: Not much, I know. Don't be discouraged; this is a temporary setback.

Eddie gets in line.

B.O.S.: All better, I see.

EDDIE: Listen.

B.O.S.: You were in shock. We stabilized you.

EDDIE: Fair is fair. I've served. And for my struggle?

B.O.S.: It's a crapshoot. *(He hands Eddie a turkey)* There's a good one: pop-up timer. Anyway, that's the price we pay . . .

EDDIE: I've served and I want my recompense.

B.O.S.: We saved your life, and this is gratitude?

EDDIE: Shit.

B.O.S.: You're holding up the line.

Eddie cannot help but feel he was tagged soft-hearted. Politics forced him out. He finds lodging in a boarding house and spends warm days on the stoop. When it is cold, he goes to the no-name bar down the street. He drinks beer and vodka, cheap off-brands, with the other men. As their money goes, men disappear. They do not understand their failure; the television set over the bar broadcasts strong numbers. Some of the men fight when they are drunk.

Eddie steers clear of trouble. He sells the jewelry, piece by piece, to an old woman who runs a pawnshop out of her apartment. Eddie does not linger. The woman's flesh and greasy strongbox, the smells of must and cabbage, drive him from the flat, his head filled with crazy ideas. Why not kill her and take the cash and valuables? They would be of more use to him than to the old miser.

X I

Eddie is on the sidewalk in a warehouse district. He stops to take a drink from the pint in his back pocket. A pickup with a leaning wooden topper pulls up. Eddie recognizes the old man on the passenger side.

The man rolls down the window. —Speak of the devil.

—You look worse than when I saw you last, Eddie says.

The Businessman of the Damned gets out of the truck. His suit, long out of style, is immaculate, and his ancient boots gleam. —And you're a pretty picture, eh, lad?

EDDIE: What the fuck do you know?

B.O.D.: Given up soldiering, but still a soldier's mouth. We like to think talent is all, yet temperament rules as well.

EDDIE: C'mon now. *(He holds out the bottle)* Hell, have a drink.

B.O.D.: Thanks, no. I'm on company time. By the way, I might have something for you.

EDDIE: Yeah?

B.O.D.: Stop by tomorrow.

Construction site surrounded by a cyclone fence. Eddie walks, looking for the gate. A group of men stands around a large table. Eddie starts toward the entrance. A guard steps from a box. The Businessman of the Damned, in orange bump cap, waves Eddie through.

EDDIE: Hello.

B.O.D.: Recognize it?

They stand on a lip of sand. A dirt road leads into a deep stone pit.

EDDIE: Long way down.

B.O.D.: Bulldozed the whole neighborhood.

EDDIE: How deep you say that is?

B.O.D.: Five hundred square acres, and over a thousand dwellings. Had 'em jammed like warrens. You remember.

EDDIE: I mean straight down.

B.O.D.: Your old haunts, eh?

EDDIE: A field, then they built over it?

B.O.D.: Once maybe. What wasn't? Field, woods, glen and dale. Sweet grass in the morning when dew clings to the blades. Ah, memory. Innocent eye in the field of green. Something in that. Yes, an appeal. No, you are not the first to have these feelings. No, sir. But how could you know? If you throw out history? Have I told you, have I bored you, with the lethal consequences of forgetfulness?

EDDIE: What place is this?

B.O.D.: The plans! Get an eyeful of those blueprints; you'll see the future.

EDDIE: Plans.

B.O.D.: Would you then go backward? Unloom the looming factory wall? Spin a wheel in some cottage? What fate, that? Beyond, to sheep on some Attic hillside?

EDDIE: Forget it.

B.O.D.: All to the good.

He leads Eddie to the table, points to the plans. Lines correspond to no scale Eddie is aware of.

B.O.D. *(Tenderly)*: You find this a bit beyond you, lad?

EDDIE: I can't.

B.O.D. *(Leading Eddie down the winding road to the pit)*: It's all right, son. Don't let it get you.

EDDIE: Maybe if I look again?

B.O.D.: It's all right. We both know the deficiencies in your education. That's no shame. If anything, I blame myself. *(Tears run down his cheeks)* The hard and lean times they were, there was not a penny to be spared.

EDDIE: Spared.

B.O.D.: I won't apologize. Don't rake me over the dead embers of yesteryear. There was always food on the table, wasn't there? Was there not? If you'd seen the rotten crusts I came to manhood upon perhaps—

Eddie stumbles, careens near the edge of the roadway, catches his balance.

B.O.D.: Quite right. Yesterday's gone and the devil take his own. I'm old.

They reach bottom: rock and sand, clumps of scrub and thistle. Eddie watches a lizard skitter under a rock. He is surprised by the heat. They walk for a long time; Eddie's sneakers fill with sand.

Men, maybe a hundred of them, move a huge slab of rock. It looks like concrete, and it is enmeshed in thick hemp cables. Foremen shout through bullhorns.

B.O.D.: Walk it, walk it.

The men pull; the slab inches forward, side-to-side.

EDDIE: Jesus Christ, it must weigh a ton.

B.O.D.: Just the thing.

EDDIE: Can't you use a machine?

B.O.D.: Sure, technology will only take you so far; it's art carries you through.

EDDIE: Oh.

B.O.D.: Imagine this a garden. Dirt, dust but momentary disruptions. But look.

The Businessman of the Damned waves his hand over the floor of the pit. The landscape is dotted with concrete slabs.

B.O.D.: Each of these—now focus, boy, picture it—each of these will be a sculpture. Each sculpture sculpted by a different sculptor. A world-famous sculptor for each.

EDDIE: A sculpture garden.

B.O.D.: The beauty.

Eddie works in the quarry, shoveling gravel. A guy tells him a lot of people started in the quarry. It is always possible to move up.

The slabs stand every fifty yards or so like giant dominoes. The pit floor is level, but when the slabs are carved and the slag hauled off, the land will be graded and landscaped. Wood-chipped paths will wind through the greenery.

Eddie thinks as he fills wheelbarrows. His job will not last forever, and the future must hold something for him. He has credentials and talent. He will get himself apprenticed to a sculptor.

The chief's trailer is padlocked. The corrugated sheds and planning table, the guards and sentry box are gone. The gate is chained and locked. Eddie goes back to the quarry. No one is there.

He has to find the others. He runs. The sun sets. The slabs glow in the moonlight. Eddie dodges around them, stumbling. He finds himself on a plain of dirt and scrub. Beer cans and a tattered yellow rain jacket glow in the moonlight. He crashes through the brush. Brambles whip his shins, wrists, face. Up a sandy rise, down again. The faint ruts of heavy equipment. Eddie follows the trail into a chain-link fence. His face hits the metal, rebounds, hits again. Eddie crumbles.

He is thirsty. Trucks used to bring ice water in plastic coolers. Enough water for ten men in each.

He walks the fence.

Sun burns hot in this hole. Something to that. Something Eddie heard long ago about the sun or fire or X rays.

The fence gives him support.

A silver band shines. Sometimes it recedes, other times it is upon him, and Eddie gasps for air.

The water runs down his neck. Eddie shakes like a wet dog. A man up ahead leans easily over a dip in the fence. His elbow is propped on the rail, and he smokes a cigarette he holds in his free hand.

Eddie cannot believe his eyes. He has been alone in this wilderness for—for a long time. Sun started to get to him after a while. Burned.

The man wears a torn jacket that is covered with insignia and ribbons, corroded medals and rotten braid. His face is weathered and cracked, the left eye gone, the socket a mass of scar tissue with indications of crude stitching. Years ago, no doubt. Now the mass is almost natural.

Eddie looks at the cigarette. —Have another? He raises his hands. —A bit to share? Perhaps a puff or two, or give me ends on it? If it's no trouble. Eddie walks in a small circle. —No trouble. No. No trouble. Trouble flies above us day and night. No. Eddie reverses himself, walks the circle backwards. —Flies above. Waiting.

—Ah, the man says. He shakes a cigarette half-free from the pack and holds it out to Eddie.

—God will repay you, Eddie says.

The man nods, gives Eddie light. —Been waiting for you.

—I don't mind saying I am moved, Eddie says.

—Part of my responsibility.

—Uh?

—I walk, the man says. Security.

—Can't make you out, Eddie says.

—I'm right here. The man takes a piece of soiled paper from his pocket. —Believe me, once you'd have known me clear as day.

The man seems to be in the shadows.

—Dark over there, Eddie says.

The man holds the paper near his good eye, squints, shakes his head, takes a magnifying glass from his pocket.

—Trouble with your eyes? Eddie says. Had trouble with mine as well.

—What? Yes. And how did it out?

—Cleared up completely.

—There we have it, the man says. He peers through the glass. —Completely? Just the thing. Let's see. It's a lot of crap. You've been appointed caretaker.

—Care?

—In recognition of your service, it says. You must be connected.

—How?

—Separate the useable material from the fill. You're certified here an expert.

—Certified expert?

—Me, too. You see me a messenger boy. Diminished capacity. But still hanging in, though I have my grievances.

The man points to his feet.

Eddie looks at the man's running shoes. They are frayed and stained, bound with tape.

—My dear father, the man says, this was years ago, was a shoemaker. In those happy days, no self-respecting man would be seen outside his own home, the sacred domicile, in brightly-colored cloth footgear, the likes of which might only be seen on women in certain quarters. Time was, a man's gear spoke a language: you got something, a cap, perhaps, of a peculiar and nonutilitarian design to speak your rank, and now—

Eddie nods. —All open to interpretation.

—No.

—Matters of opinion.

—A fact, the man says, is a fact.

—Cul, Eddie says, cul.

—Culturally determined paradigms. Christ, don't pull that old saw on me.

—I don't want to pull anything, Eddie says.

—I had a message. I gave you the message. Will you stop this relentless interrogation? What do you want from me?

—Well, Eddie says. I mean—

—Inadequate, the man says. Inadequate.

—All I want, Eddie says.

—All right, the man says. I have this job. My side of the fence. A monumental garden of memory. Valley of the Fallen. I watch to be sure no one disturbs it. All I could get, this. This, and they gave me some language.

Eddie finds a broken spade in a heap of burnt cans. He works from sunrise to sunset shoveling the styrofoam cups and plastic sheeting and paper and glass into piles. It is hopeless.

The full moon rises. Wolves and coyotes howl. Eddie needs a fire, but there is no wood on his side of the fence. On the other side, the sandy plain gives way to tree-covered hills.

Eddie goes over the fence, crawls across the plain, creeps up a hill. A voice whistles through the trees.

The security man stands surrounded by statuary in a dale. Eddie sees the flat, milky squares set in the turf.

—Look homeward, the man says. If it is here, it is everywhere, and the corollary applies as well.

Eddie thinks the man is talking to a sculpted soldier, but the man turns to a miniature granite house with lions guarding the entrance.

—Dark or light, the man says, it's all guilt. I get by. Nobody gives you anything. Make of it what you will. And you stones nodding. Always nodding. There's no escape. All theory aside.

. . .

The slabs are useable, and since Eddie cannot move them, he mounds fill at the slabs' bases and numbers the slabs with a bit of charred wood. He draws up a key.

There are some pieces, really quality material, that Eddie holds out. He uses a hard rock. Trial and error. Crude figurines. In time he learns the secret faults and methodologies of flaking and shaping. He makes women. The forms are round, tending towards circularity. Squat, plump women.

The larger pieces, three-quarters lifesize, are made in components and cemented together. Each piece is based on Dolores. Sometimes Eddie doubts his imagination. He sculpts her with the birds of the air. The birds form a circle at her feet, and some of the delicate creatures perch on her outstretched arms. Eddie is not sure if he has got it right.

He spaces the pieces in a long oval: Dolores and the birds; eating at a table; pushing a broom; in ecstasy; at the beach; teaching a child; reading; to the centerpiece, where Dolores stands alone and serene in imagined moonlight; descending to Dolores burying the dead; drinking wine; smoking a cigarette; sleeping; walking in a garden; and rising from her bath, the water beading on her breasts.

Eddie is almost finished when the security man comes back.

—This is it? the man says.

Eddie turns from his work. —Not quite done.

—I am, the man says.

—Finished?

—Papers came through today.

—Good?

—Best news in a hell of a while. The man lights a cigarette stub. —There it is. Imported. Saved this for a bit.

—Oh.

—All things in the fullness of time.

—Yeah.

—Every dog his moment in the sun.

—Think so?

—Hard work and perseverance. Deferred gratification. Don't teach that in the schools.

—No.

—I can see, the man says, from what you've done, that you're capable of work. Direction went a bit wrong, I'll grant that, but you'll be fine.

—Thanks.

—I have something for you.

Eddie follows him over the fence. A glen. Stream runs swiftly over rocks, foam building in the eddies. They walk a game trail to the water's edge.

—I remember, Eddie says, his eyes filling with tears. A place like this.

The man ducks under a bush. —Coming?

Eddie crawls after him. Small insects hover. Eddie inhales a few. He tries to keep the man in sight, but sweat runs into his eyes, and it is all flashes of light and the quick animal sounds of the man's forward motion.

A clearing.

—The old long haul, the man says.

Eddie gets up.

—Worth the effort. The man points.

A hut that looks like a cross between a geodesic dome and a yurt. The materials are eclectic—wooden beams, sheet metal, flattened cans, fiberboard, plastic sheeting, paper-mâché. Bracelets, necklaces, earrings, crucifixes, rings, beads, pictures, dolls, mirrors, bottles, rosaries, candlesticks, statues, etchings, and other objects hang from the shed. Parts of the hut shine brilliantly; other parts are dull and rotting.

—Very special thing, the man says, this.

—Where did it come from?

—Would you believe I built it, or that it's always been here? In one form or another.

Eddie chuckles politely.

—Well, it's yours now.

—Mine?

—Don't bother to thank me. The pleasure's in handing it on.

—I, Eddie says.

—You'll be safe here. The man walks Eddie around the hut. —Each has its power. And what's underneath. It's solid.

Eddie looks through a window. The dirty glass has been lined with foil.

—If only my family had stayed.

—The foil, Eddie says.

—Fucking rays. The man gestures toward some beads and feathers. —Break up the patterns.

—Huh, Eddie says.

—Used to laugh at me. Theoretical. Now they're coming faster and faster. Through the hole. Experts agree.

—Good idea.

—I'd give you the keys, but there's no lock. Very safe out here. Far from the prying eye. The man unbuckles his pistol belt and hands it to Eddie. —Take this.

—You sure?

—Go ahead, open it.

Eddie unsnaps the holster. Instead of the regulation forty-five, there is a cheap twenty-five in oily wax paper.

—It's not original, Eddie says.

—You'll probably never use it. Just in case.

When the light starts to go, Eddie makes his way back to the clearing. Sleep comes easily.

He never disturbs the walls or floor or foil. The bones of of Lost Kings have hardened and become encrusted with jewels. His statues are finished. He spends his days digging for the bones which will erase the past. Eddie finds buried things.

The sun gets to him. It seems that everything that has

happened to him is happening. But nothing will affect him as long as he searches for the bones.

He wakes, choking, crawls across the floor, outside. The woods are on fire. Heat waves shimmer above the trees. He stands. The flames move toward the hut. Eddie sees a figure through the trees. Fritz ignites the woods with a flame-thrower. The trenches Eddie has dug act as a firebreak.

—Shut it down, Eddie calls.

Fritz switches the thrower off. —What?

—You're going to burn my house.

—House? Fritz walks through the network of trenches to Eddie. He wears a black asbestos apron, and a welder's visor is tilted back on his head. —You have a house? Impossible.

Eddie points to the hut.

Fritz lights a cigarette and shakes his head. —This isn't in the plan.

—I live here.

—Off the charts, Fritz says.

—Since I fell by the wayside, Eddie says, it seems as though my voice has been drowned out. I talk and talk; it is, I think, a long scream, although no one seems to hear. Perhaps you think they don't hear because they have no interest in hearing a laundry list of gripes, but I think they do hear, as gibberish and nothing.

Fritz looks at his cigarette. —You want one of these?

—Please, Eddie says.

Fritz hands him a cigarette, gives him a light with a shiny Zippo. —Enjoy the break. Then I better do the shack.

—You can't.

—Look at yourself, man. You had something once; now we find you howling like a dog on a chain.

—I should be destroyed, Eddie says. His right hand drifts to his side.

—Suit yourself, Fritz says.

Eddie takes the twenty-five from the holster, steps quick,

jams the muzzle of the pistol under Fritz's chin. —Talk talk talk talk.

—We thought you were going to be a nice guy about this.

Eddie hears someone behind him. —Move and I'll blow his head off.

—Predictable, Fritz says.

—Nice trenches, the Businessman of the Saved says. From above, they form a sort of constellation. Bird or bear or something.

The Businessman of the Saved looks at the pistol. —Pretty puny. That thing won't protect you forever.

EDDIE: Just another minute.

B.O.S.: Ad infinitum?

EDDIE: Give me a chance to show what I can do.

B.O.S.: You're an ornament at best. Oh, don't pout. Lower the gun; I'll get you something.


Eddie gets the concession to the sculpture garden and the talisman hut. Fritz clears off the woods. The trenches are billed as ancient outerspace etchings. Eddie's statues are replaced with colorful fiberglass replicas. He will wear a blazer, slacks, tie. The company provides the uniform, stocks the gift shop, provides a trailer.

The crowds are pretty good. Plump, sunburned families who stop for pictures: the kids climbing on the hut, Dad with his arm around Dolores as she rises from the bath. Local antiquaries with guidebooks. Teachers with their classes from the community college.

The visitors drop off. Blank pages in the guest book. Eddie never knows how much popcorn to pop or how many hot dogs to put in the roto-griller. The people who do come are strange. Women with thick accents and prayerbooks. Men clutching manuscripts. Two teenage boys with a telescope and sextant bring Eddie a case of Mexican beer. Eddie is forbidden to accept gratuities, but he takes the beer.

The Businessman of the Saved stops by. Eddie is showing

the garden to a retired dentist. When the tour is finished, Eddie and the Businessman of the Saved walk.

B.O.S.: Sculpture gardens are white elephants.

EDDIE: What does it profit you to close?

B.O.S.: Sculpture, pit, it's all the same.

EDDIE: Pit?

B.O.S.: We made some power, we got some waste. Way of the world. We can't change it.

EDDIE: Power? Waste?

B.O.S.: Creates it. Law of nature. Nice idea, but it's out of my hands. We all have our limits.

EDDIE: I was commissioned.

B.O.S.: Assigned. Make-work proposition.

EDDIE: And?

B.O.S.: Hell of a headache, but it worked out. Turns out to be a perfect storage site. Later, who knows? Maybe an aquarium. Or some kind of multiplex.

XII

A rig hauls Eddie's trailer to a wooded area far from the main gate. In Eddie's place they put up a cinderblock building. Eddie asks a workman what it is. The guy says it is a pumphouse. That is where Eddie hangs, waiting to see if they will have something for him. The security men will not let him inside. Eddie looks at himself on the closed-circuit monitor at the checkpoint. They give him an application and lend him a ballpoint and correction fluid. He has a problem with the address blank. He puts *on site*. Position desired: *any*.

The security chief looks at Eddie's form.

—You think they'll have something?

The man shrugs.

—When will I hear?

—Thank you for your interest in the firm.

Eddie waits each day. The security men ignore him. Some of the other employees say hello. Eddie takes their cordiality as a good sign. The employees are well-dressed. Eddie knows he must dress as who he wants to be. He makes sure to put on his necktie, and he never carries a lunch. Someday he will get an umbrella and carry that. He waits in the heat of the day by the soda machine.

A woman in labcoat and eyeglasses talks to Eddie. She works in the pumphouse.

—Running the pumps? Eddie says.

—Not like you think.

—Oh, Eddie says, I understand.

—It's all monitored.

—Yes, yes.

—Electronically, you know, by computers.

—You watch the computers?

—The graphics. On a screen.

—If the pump breaks, you fix it? Or the pipes? You know how to fix pipes?

—The crews do that.

—So, Eddie says, so to get in, I don't have to know how to fix pipes?

—It depends on your classification.

—Yeah.

—There are different jobs.

—I understand, Eddie says.

—Don't give up, the woman says.

At night, Eddie thinks about the pumphouse. Not what the name implies, he knows. He pictured the place as a damp, dark area crisscrossed with pipes, valves, gauges, catwalks. Now he knows it is cool and clean. Carpeted. Fluorescent lighting. Quiet. The technicians sit at their tables, watching the screens. Colored lines trace the water's progress through the system. The network of pipes and pumps is buried deep underground in bunker-like tunnels.

. . .

The head guard comes to the soda machine. —This is not helping you.

—I'm ready and available, Eddie says.

—I sent your paper along. Takes time to go through channels. You will be contacted.

—I know that.

—You got to get out of here. The guard hands Eddie a ticket. —Go down front and take the tour.

The central administrative complex is really something: a thirty-story glass-and-steel octagon with neo-something cornices and archways and a giant clock set at the apex. Inside, gloved Courtesy Girls greet the tourists and offer tea, cookies, towelettes. The offices are large and airy with simulated wood floors so durable, the guide says, they could not be damaged with a blowtorch. There are Oriental carpets and wet bars and streamlined desks and copier rooms and atria and departments: Sales, Training, Documentation, Promotion, Internal Communications, Security, Production, Human Resources, and many more.

The grounds are even better. There are brooks and organic sculptures and stone benches and alabaster cherubs and goddesses and groves of fruit trees and reflecting pools and rock gardens.

A man in coveralls prunes a pear tree.

—Funny, Eddie says.

—What?

—You trim artificial trees?

—They're real.

Eddie looks around. —Doesn't it freeze in the winter?

—No, not when controlled with climate-sensitive implants and micro-botanical pumps. The chips tell them how to grow.

Eddie moves along, takes in the storage silos, heavy-equipment sheds, independent installations. He likes the cooling pools, the long azure rectangles that recall postcard canals.

. . .

Word is Eddie better keep away from the pumphouse. There is a time for retrenchment. Eddie stays in the trailer and writes long letters to whom it may concern, stating the facts of his case. Although he knows he must go to the top, Eddie does not want to seem unreasonable. He states his preference for a slot in the pumphouse. Any position will do. But he is careful to indicate that he understands such a plum may not immediately come his way. Eddie suggests that some of the free space on-site could be used as a civic center where athletes and other performers could put on spectacular programs of entertainment. This would not only increase civic feeling, it would also create jobs, permanent employment for ushers, concession-stand workers, cleaning people, etc.

He waits when the shifts change and catches the workers. He holds the sheaf of letters like a stack of pamphlets. Most employees pass without looking at him, but a few politely accept the blotted sheets of notebook paper.

The woman emerges from the crowd. —I wondered what happened to you.

—Still here, Eddie says. They won't dislodge me.

—That's good.

—Determination is half the battle, Eddie says. Well, determination and enthusiasm.

—I see.

—You can't rule out enthusiasm, Eddie says.

—Great attitude, the woman says.

—I visualize myself a success, Eddie says. I think it's really helping. Every day, I feel better and better.

Someone pounds on the trailer's door. Eddie jumps up. His first impulse is to go for a weapon. —Coming, he says.

He opens the door.

Fritz stands on the cinderblock that serves as a stoop.

—You? Eddie says.

—Let me in, Fritz says.

Eddie stands aside.

—Nice, Fritz says. He folds the converted bed into the wall, pulls out the legs, and it becomes the dining table. —Seen worse. Shit, lived in worse.

—What do you want?

—They asked me to talk to you. Your letter went up the chain. Now you got results.

—Which one?

Fritz shrugs. —Who knows? Your plea's been heard, right? That's what you wanted, right? Sometimes, frankly, I wonder about the clarity of people's objectives. Read any of those books about how to prioritize?

—Books?

—Doesn't matter. Check your TV set. They have these people on periodically. I know what you want—you want to get inside. Everybody wants in—you need to cling to something.

—No problem, Eddie says.

—But these letters, Fritz says, this out-there thing, this here-I-am-world. I don't think so. If you're a nut case and you want attention, okay, you got it. But I hate to let it go that way.

—What I want, Eddie says, is to show what I can do.

—We're fully aware of what you're capable of. By the way, are you in the possession of any firearms?

—Of course not.

—I want you to think of me as a friend, Fritz says. But to be honest with you, pal, you are barking up the wrong tree. You got some coffee or something?

—Instant okay?

—My favorite.

Eddie pops two mugs of water in the microwave.

—I understand, Fritz says. I've been where you're at.

—Uh huh, Eddie says.

He spoons the crystals into the mugs, stirs, waits to hear more.

. . .

Someone shoves a letter under the door of Eddie's trailer. It says he is to report to Central Administration so he can be a member of the floating pool. Eddie reports. He is given white paint, pans, rollers.

—When you've covered that one, see me, the supervisor says. I'll have something else for you.

They follow a concrete path to the orchards. Eddie steers the woman from the pumphouse onto a woodchip-covered trail that leads to a moon-viewing platform overlooking a rock garden. The air is heavy with the sweet perfume of ripening fruit. Golden mechanical birds sing unearthly melodies in the trees. Colors swirl in the half light. Lemons and oranges are imbued with sensual flesh tones, cherries and plums take on deep and rich hues. Eddie notices the iridescent sheen of the woman's black dress, the heavy, smooth sway of her movements. As they begin to ascend to the viewing platform, he reaches for her hand. It flutters like a tiny bird until it rests securely in the steely trap of Eddie's grasp.

She lets out a low moan. —Oh, God.

Eddie strokes her hair, guides her to a bench. The moon shines over the rock garden.

—Marry me, Eddie gasps.

### XIII

Things pick up. Eddie goes to the head of the department, a young woman named Linda.

—What can you do? Linda says.

—Hmm, Eddie says.

—In terms of the department?

Eddie puts his best foot forward.

Linda smiles vaguely, nods. —Impressive. Unfortunately, we have a staff of much more qualified people. No reflection on you; it's just that we have so many exceptional candidates.

—I understand.

—I'll give you what I can.

—You won't regret it. I need the work. I'm thinking of starting a family.

They give him a selection of brushes and six colors in an oil-based product he has never used.

—Two things, the supervisor says. Get the slogan in, and give the finished product a few coats of varnish. That's for your durability.

Eddie nods and carries his equipment up the ladder to the billboard. He does a brilliant sky, fluffy clouds, radiant sun, and arcs the words AQUARIUM OF THE FUTURE across it. Eddie works in hills with neatly-shaped cypress trees. Although he has not seen the plans, he paints the aquarium as a giant swimming pool with three concrete walls and a glass front. Fish, squid, sharks, and barracudas contend in the water. The picture is glossy, professionally done. Still, a bit cold. Needs something. He puts a brontosaurus in the water. Pterodactyls fly overhead. A mastodon grazes on a hillside.

A secretary shows him into the office. Eddie slumps in the chair and says he will have coffee. It is all over. There are studies of canals on the walls. To be built with the future in mind. Now that he is X'd out, Eddie feels pain and guilt and loss. Opportunities, he sees, were placed before him on a silver platter, but he never capitalized on them because he lived his life wrong, with no direction or thought. Now the canals will be built without him, and who can say what green and pleasant land will spring forth here?

A man in a suit comes in.

Eddie rises.

—Don't get up. The man shakes Eddie's hand. —Sorry I'm late. He looks at Eddie's coffee cup. —I see you've been taken care of. Good. There's a trend nowadays to refuse all offered beverages. Frankly, I don't like it.

Eddie slumps back in his chair.

—In China, for example, somebody wants to talk business, what's he offer you?

—I don't know, Eddie says.

—Cup of tea and a cigarette. You think you refuse either one? Not if you want to do business.

—What have you got to lose? Eddie says.

The man chuckles. —Indeed. He opens a manila folder. —You've intersected with some top people. Impressive.

—Thanks.

—May I speak off the record?

Eddie nods.

—I've received a call or calls on your behalf from a certain party or parties.

—Great.

—Great, and not so great. We like to think a clearly-defined chain of command is the hallmark of an efficient operation. And we are an efficient operation.

—Yeah?

—The kind of immediate access you are used to is a thing of the past. Bottom line: We're a joint governmental/private sector initiative with a specific mission. Can you see yourself fitting into that sort of structure?

—Sure, Eddie says. In fact, I've got some ideas. I've been doing the billboards—designing a logo, really, like a basic model, but I think I could expand on it. Put some people in the picture, some world leaders maybe, and some women, and a dog. Something that'll catch on. Then kick it—on T-shirts, coffee mugs, posters—you know. Push it and push it. Push as hard as the market will bear. That's success. Do you agree?

The form says Eddie is in the Promotions Department, but he has to report to the gym. A towel boy tells him the trainer is busy teaching low-impact aerobics. Eddie has a look around. Basketball court with a well-surfaced track running around the upper level, weight rooms with computer-assisted machines, Olympic pool, saunas, locker rooms. He keeps his eyes open for heavy and speed bags. Eddie cannot find any.

—You the guy Thompson called about? the trainer says.

—I guess. Eddie follows the man into an office.

—What I see, the trainer says, is low body fat, but equally low muscle mass. Skinny. You smoke?

—Need one?

—Quit. You'll need lung capacity. Drink?

—Well . . .

—Quit. The trainer gives Eddie a pamphlet. —Follow the diet and use a multi-vitamin. Run. Two miles a day. Build up to ten. Strength is the big problem.

—I may not look like much, Eddie says, but I can handle myself in a pinch.

—Yeah, yeah, the trainer says.

Eddie trains hard. The work pays off. He breathes easier. His troubles are gone. Eddie feels strong as a bull.

They treat him like a king. Beautiful women approach offering food and drink. Eddie looks at their hair and athletic suits and does not know what to say. There are cables and cameras, generators and lights, even a small crane.

Thompson greets Eddie. —You know what we need. Just swim the canal. Don't worry about the rest.

—Yeah, Eddie says, I got it.

—Just jump in the water and swim.

—Okay. There's one thing, though, I have my doubts about. A little problem.

Thompson stiffens. —Doubts, no.

—More of a question, really.

—Fine. Whatever you need to know.

—It's only a hundred yards?

—Good question. We welcome questions, particularly good ones.

A whistle blows.

—You have to go, man.

Eddie walks to the edge of the canal. Two production assistants slip the robe from his body. The trainer massages his shoulders and neck, whispers in his ear.

Eddie stands at the edge.

Dives.

XIV

Eddie and Deirdre are married in the company chapel. Mr. Thompson and Mr. Thompson's lovely wife, Mrs. Thompson, serve as witnesses. There is a small reception in the basement of the chapel. Most of those in attendance are friends of the bride. Mr. Thompson presents Eddie with some envelopes that acquaintances in the firm have sent. Eddie puts them in his jacket for later.

Deirdre would like a honeymoon in Paris or Rome. Eddie favors the Yucatan or Tahiti. This is not to be. The newlyweds are needed at work. Mr. Thompson has booked them a honeymoon suite at a suburban hotel. It is the least he can do, Mr. Thompson says.

Best of all is the house, a brand new two-bedroom in the company development, Garden Groves. Eddie and Deirdre are able to get it with almost nothing down through a special program. The rate is very favorable, and the payments are automatically deducted from their wages.

Eddie and Deirdre go out to look the place over. Eddie determines the construction is sound. The living room is done in faux Chippendale, the dining room has a sturdy walnut table and captain's chairs, the kitchen appliances are energy-efficient. It is all perfect.

In the bedroom, Deirdre is sprawled on the fourposter bed. Eddie sits in the country French rocker.

—Come here, Deirdre says. I have something for you.

Deirdre takes him by the hand and leads him downstairs, down another flight to the basement. There a laundry area and a storeroom and a room that is refinished as a den with a roll-top desk, Victorian couch, bookcases, and antique globe.

—All this, Eddie says, his voice trembling.

Happy are their days. At work, Deirdre is promoted, although Eddie is not sure what she is promoted to. It is technical. Eddie is made swimmaster at the aquarium, just as Mr. Thompson promised he would be. The dolphins and killer whales arrive with specially-trained special trainers, another married couple. They are handsome people—blond and tan in their neoprene wetsuits. They run the spectacles and swims they erroneously call fish shows. Everyone knows dolphins and killer whales are aquatic mammals, as Eddie is tempted to point out. But it is not too bad. Eddie has an athletic suit and cap with his title on them and a chrome whistle and expensive-looking plastic sandals. He carries a clipboard and makes sure no one is in danger and no one drowns.

He stops at the Humane Society after work. More variety than he expected. Tiers of steel cages, concrete floor with drain, the smell of animals and feed. Eddie grabs a puppy and signs the papers. An attendant puts the dog in a box that folds shut. Deirdre loves the puppy from the moment she opens the box. She rushes out to get it food and dog bowls and chew bones and toys and a cedar-filled pet bed.

—What's he called? Deirdre says.

—You decide, Eddie says.

Each evening, as they lie entwined in each other's arms in the fourposter, Deirdre says, Bobby, or Henry, or Herman, or Jesse, or Frank.

Eddie says, it is up to you.

Eddie converts the storage room to a home workshop. He makes a pegboard holder and hangs his newly-purchased tools from it. He buys a workbench kit and assembles it. When the bench is finished, Eddie stains the raw pine a rich color and bolts a big metal vise to it.

His first real project is building a house for the dog. Eddie gets the plans from a woodworking magazine and goes to the lumber yard for plywood, screws, nails, tarpaper, glue.

The doghouse takes no time. Eddie places it at the base of one of the clothespoles and steps back to admire his work. The shiny rows of nailheads gleam on the tarpaper roof. The dog sniffs the house, barks, runs away. Deirdre calls and whistles, tells the dog he is a good boy, tries to coax him into the doghouse. The dog sits looking at Deirdre, his tongue hanging out of his mouth.

—He needs to get used to it, Eddie says.

Eddie steps behind the dog and grabs its collar. He pulls the dog to its feet and tries to drag it to the doghouse. The dog snarls, twists his head, snaps at Eddie's wrist.


Calls start coming at all hours of the night. The princess phone rings. Eddie reaches over and grabs it.

—Will you shut that dog up? a man says. He is keeping my kids awake.

—Okay, Eddie says.

The calls come every night. When Eddie tries to tell the caller that it must be another dog, the caller becomes agitated, shouts obscenities, threatens to telephone the authorities.

Eddie stops after work and gets a big, heavy muzzle. He takes the muzzle out of the bag. Deirdre backs away.


A dark figure with a long gun runs across the lawn. Deirdre screams. The figure turns and fires. Eddie dives, forces Deirdre down onto the grass. A second gunman somewhere. Eddie observes the graceful arc of tracer fire against the dark suburban sky. He tries to shield Deirdre. But Deirdre wriggles out from under him. Eddie reaches for her wrist but catches the knife blade instead. Deirdre pulls away, leaving Eddie with a long gash across the palm of his hand. He sees her lunge at the dark figure. The figure fires and Deirdre goes down. Eddie rolls to the doghouse and fires from behind it. The figure stumbles, drops the long gun, pulls out a short one. Eddie hears another gun. Eddie's ammo runs out. The sun comes up. Automatic lawn sprinklers come on.

XV

An extraordinarily bright day, the day of Deirdre's funeral, and the glare bothers Eddie. Everything—the shiny hearse and limousines, the marble tombstones, the hard, cloudless sky, even the nitrogen-enriched grass—reflects some terrible light and leaves Eddie feeling dull and weak. Some kind of minister stands at the graveside. Their marriage was so short, their time together so sweet and fleeting, he never asked what her religious affiliation, if any, was.

When the glare is too much, Eddie closes his eyes. He could faint, but Eddie does not feel faint. People do faint, he knows. Perfectly normal. A sign of strong emotion or even identification. Not for him. Eddie opens his eyes. The minister closes his book.

People drift away. Some pause to shake Eddie's hand and murmur a few words of solace. Eddie knows what to do. He nods and softly says *thank you.* Mr. Thompson comes over, hand outstretched.

—Terrible thing, Mr. Thompson says.

—Thank you, Eddie says.

—Don't worry. It's all buried. Nobody will ever know.

—Know?

—You are safe. Garden Groves is coming down anyway.

—Thank you, Eddie says.

—All on a toxic dump. Bulldoze it and let her sit for a while. Monitor the site.

—That's a great comfort to me, Eddie says.

—Put up something else. After she cools down. You may be able to help.

Eddie nods solemnly and greets other mourners until someone ushers him to a car.

. . .

The car brings Eddie to company headquarters. Two men in dark suits greet him and take him to a room in the basement. There are a table and three wooden chairs.

—Sit, one man says.

The other man drops a package of cigarettes and a book of matches on the table. —Go ahead.

Eddie opens the pack and takes a cigarette.

—Comfortable?

Eddie nods.

—All right. The man straddles one of the chairs.

The other man sits facing Eddie. —Let's get going. I'm Bob, and this is Jim. We're your friends in the company. Your legal advisors, you might say.

They interrogate Eddie for twenty hours.


Eddie is given a small room with a single bed, dresser, and sink. The toilet and shower stalls are down the hall. A woman brings him food in styrofoam trays.

Everything is explained. Eddie cannot go home. The house is sealed. It may be best not to see the place again. Put the past behind him. The company gives him a small settlement for his possessions and equity.

Eddie has no duties; the company is giving him some time for readjustment. He spends his days in the lounge at the end of the hall, watching television.

A game show is on when Mr. Thompson comes in. —I tried your room.

Eddie turns off the TV. —Just killing time.

—Climbing the walls, huh? Mr. Thompson hands Eddie a plastic shopping bag. —I brought you a few things.

Eddie nods and looks in the bag: razor, toothbrush, cigarettes, lighter, and other items. Eddie weeps. He sobs. His shoulders shake. His nose runs.

—Easy, Mr. Thompson says. Now, now.

—Thank you. Thank you so much.

—Not at all. Now get a hold of yourself.

Eddie shakes his head. —It's too late.

—Be a man. I hate to say it, but that's what it comes down to. In the end, that's all there is.

—For what? What does it profit me?

—You can't go on like this.

Eddie clutches his head. —My world is dark. Dark.

—We must go on. Terrible thing that happened. And other things, believe it or not, just as terrible. Happening now. Or yet to happen.

—You see, Eddie says.

—I try to remember, Mr. Thompson says, that we will all die just as dead as the dead are now, someday.

—Does it help? Eddie weeps harder.

Mr. Thompson takes the handkerchief from his breast pocket. —Take it. I think you need something. Maybe a raise.

—Can hold me, Eddie says, but it's coming. Believe me, it is coming.

Mr. Thompson backhands Eddie so hard that Eddie is knocked halfway out of his chair. —You're a lucky man.

—Lucky?

—You are not at the bottom. Nowhere close. In fact, you're nearer the top. Take a look down there; it's hell.

Eddie wipes his face with the handkerchief.

—We need to get you back in the swing of things. My wife has a sister who's recently divorced . . .

Eddie works in an office coding documents. The work is simple, matching up numbers, mostly, but it requires a dogged concentration. When he is able to surrender completely to the numbers, he finds peace. Eddie thanks Mr. Thompson for the work.

He begins to watch his coworkers. And then to make a few notes. The notes grow into dossiers. He keeps the dossiers in his room, hidden, to the extent they can be, in the closet. None of the subjects is identified by name in the dossiers; Eddie assigns them numbers.

People are not fools. They will not jeopardize their livelihoods by committing major infractions at work. Performance is the last thing to go. But there is hearsay. People talk a great deal, and the talk in the department is very loose.

It is the private things, the private, sexual things, that interest Eddie.

—You need to get out, Mr. Thompson says.

Sunday. They are in the lounge. Eddie is watching a program about cookware.

—Out?

—You look blue.

—Blue?

—Green around the gills.

—I don't feel—

—You've been cooped up too long.

—I'm not sure.

—A supervised visit.

Mr. Thompson drives. Eddie lies blindfolded on the floor in back. Mr. Thompson warns him repeatedly not to get up or make unnecessary movement.

Eddie groans. His knees are drawn up to his chest, and the car turns again and again.

The car stops. Eddie hears a door slam. Mr. Thompson opens the back door. —Sit up. Open your eyes slowly; you'll get used to the light.

Eddie tries to roll up into a ball. Mr. Thompson is surprisingly strong. He forces Eddie up on the back seat.

—Let go, Eddie says.

Mr. Thompson slaps him. —Quit whining, baby.

Eddie opens his mouth.

Mr. Thompson hits him again.

. . .

The store is bright. Eddie stumbles and slides.

Mr. Thompson takes him by the arm. —Sorry about the rough stuff.

—Don't mention it.

—Let Deirdre go.

—Please, Eddie says, never speak her name.

—I understand. Mr. Thompson takes a list from inside his jacket. —I'll let you shop around.

Eddie wanders through the aisles. He looks at rows of work boots, drifts through housewares to sporting goods. The guns are locked in glass cabinets. The ammunition is in a case behind the counter. A young man sells some bullets to an elderly woman and steps over to the gun cabinet to show her a bolt action twenty-two rifle. Eddie leans on the counter. The ammunition cabinet is still open, glass door slid away, keys dangling in the stainless lock. Eddie steps quickly behind the counter and grabs a box of .25 ACP rounds. The clerk is showing the woman how to remove the bolt from the rifle. Eddie opens the box, spills cartridges onto the floor. The clerk looks.

Eddie crouches and begins picking up the cartridges. —Sorry. I was trying to see if these were the right kind.

—I'll take care of it, the clerk says.

Eddie puts the box on the counter.


Eddie knows his room has been searched. The files are intact. He wonders if the searchers copied the dossiers.


—We have a project for you, Mr. Thompson says. Posters. We are quite excited about this. These posters will go out in schools to the young people. The company feels that by giving young people posters with positive messages—well, you know, the benefits are obvious.

. . .

A small, windowless room on a lower level. Drafting table, chair, wastebasket, art supplies. No phone. Eddie works on some sketches. He has some idea what they want. Drugs, for example. The bad side. That is the point, Eddie thinks, of education, to make the bad side so clear, so true-to-life, that there can be no doubt what is waiting for you.

Eddie looks through the dusty sketches in the OUT box. All wrong. Days pass. Eddie works, the floor of the office ankle-deep in rejected studies, until he gets a poster right: an angular, idealized nude couple locked in a passionate embrace beneath the legend PEOPLE NEED TO BREED.

Mr. Thompson sits at the drafting table. —Hello.
—Hello.
—Saw your picture, Ed.
—And?
—We have a little problem.
—No.
—A misunderstanding. Mr. Thompson gets up and walks around the room. —What is the story behind this?
—There isn't any story, Eddie says.
—We expected a more traditional approach. The virtues of civic virtue, something like that. But there's no story, right? You said that. You just said there is no story here.
—Well—
—I'll get the story. They'll get you in a room and tell you the story.
—If that's the way it is, Eddie says.
—I saw a program on TV, Mr. Thompson says, about some happy people. They worked hard and they played hard. Why? Because they knew how to live.

Bob and Jim take Eddie to an interrogation room. A mirror on one wall.

—Why don't you give it to us again, Jim says.

—I told you, Eddie says. Told you it all.

—Tell him one more time, Bob says.

—I can't talk about it, Eddie says.

—Scary, huh? Bob says.

—You know what's scary, Jim says, is people in cars. You're in a parking ramp or walking down the street, and you see these people sitting in cars. Not doing anything. Watching. Watching for what, you have to think.

—We have had some reports, Bob says.

—These things come in threes, Jim says. Tell us everything you know.

—What are your dreams? Bob says.

—A little house with a subcompact in front? Jim says.

Bob laughs. —Can't have been much of a life in Garden Groves with—

Eddie stands up. —Don't speak their names.

—Easy, Jim says. We live in town. Fashionable area. What films do you see?

—Mooooovies? Bob says.

—Quit the fucking routine, Eddie says.

—And do what? Jim says. Talk about the weather? Sporting events? Maybe the economy? We know you too well for that. Since we're alone here, I could tell you the story of my life. My childhood, that unhappy, cramped house, the experiences that formed me. The deaths of my pets. The cruelties of my family. The sense that we were missing out on something, not just the new cars and wall-to-wall carpeting and boats and ponies and swimming pools and motor bikes, but some human reality whose absence left me hurt and empty. We could begin with my earliest memory, the sunlight in the garden, and work through every hurt and slight to the dysfunction and nigh inevitable breakup of the family.

—Nothing, Bob says, is more boring than other people's stories.

The wall around the mirror swings open. Mr. Thompson walks in. —Hold it right there.

Eddie starts to cough. He wheezes, bends over in his chair.

—Things seem to have gotten off track, Mr. Thompson says. You've lost your focus.

Eddie takes the pistol out of his sock. He sits straight up, says, —Blip, blip, blip—and fires three times.

Bob and Jim are each hit in the chest. Mr. Thompson is shot through his open mouth.

—Terrible thing, Eddie says, terrible thing.

### X V I

Eddie flies over the interstate in a giant Oldsmobile. The pressure is off. He has the car and nine hundred dollars.

Eddie will bury the past. He will burn the car across the country. Head south where it is warm all the time. Lose the Olds in a swamp.

Now it is fast food from the drive-thrus, and beer and ice when he stops for fuel. A styrofoam cooler on the back seat.

Eddie will settle in a city on the coast. Get a place near the water. Work. A job where people do not ask questions. Not much. Place, job, life. Pure and simple.

He is plagued by memories. Dreams. He leaves the lights on when he sleeps. He wakes in strange motels. Eddie jumps up, runs to the bathroom, splashes water on his face. He trembles a bit. But it stops after a while.

Eddie drives over long, flat stretches. His mind wanders. He sees himself in the future with a happy home. A companion. Soul mate. A happy family.

Eddie catches himself. —Wake up, he says. He fears he may not be able to stay awake.

His thoughts are nothing. Eddie keeps his pistol handy.

Usually, he catches the last billboarded motel before the chains, but before he knows it, he is downtown. Eddie crosses the city, finds a place on the far side of the beltway.

He is being followed. Three men in a luxury sedan. The men wear suits. Their haircuts are neat; their ties are knotted. Businessmen. Awake and aware. Working. Watching.

Eddie exits at a tourist court with an arctic motif—each cabin a mock igloo. The sedan stays on the freeway. Nerves.


They are after him. In threes or twos or ones. As many as grains of sand on a beach. Two in a Volvo outside the igloo. Three in a cargo van across a flat state.

Eddie sweats in the lunch line of a fried chicken drive-thru, ten-dollar bill in one hand, his twenty-five in the other. He is boxed. They could blip him clean. Man steps around the corner of the building, sprays and prays, Eddie is waxed. He should have thought.

Nobody comes around. The food smells good. Moist fat seeps through the bottom of the cardboard box. Eddie swings the car around and heads north.


No more drive-thrus. He fills a thermal mug with coffee at gas stations. Throws ice water from the cooler in his face when he is about to drop off.

Eddie heads for the neighborhoods he knew best. His hair has grown long and unkempt; Eddie ties it back with a strip of motel towel. He cleans his pistol with his toothbrush, carves the letter D in the wooden stock, keeps the weapon in the pocket of his work shirt.


He thinks he remembers a place where everything lost is found. Or where something was lost. Or the king lived there. He cannot keep it straight. But there is a place. Places cannot disappear. There is a law to that effect, a law of nature.

There is a wide avenue: strip mall on one side, fast food outlets on the other. Beyond the plastic roofs, a subdivision stretches over gently rolling hills. Swimming pools sparkle like gems in the sunset.

Eddie stops at a pizza place. He has to wait for a table. The families in the lobby are neat. They have straight white teeth. Eddie is embarrassed. More families crowd in behind him. He looks at some fliers on the wall.

Eddie sees the face, grainy and aged, bloated on the shoddy bill for self-defense training, glaring out above the address and phone number.


Eddie knocks. The house is a rambler with attached garage.

The door swings open.

—What can I do you for? Fritz says. He stiffens and his right hand shoots out.

Eddie jumps back, lands in a defensive posture.

—Huh, Fritz says, afraid of your own shadow?

Eddie steps forward and sticks out his hand.

Fritz takes it. —Guess we all are, on closer examination. How the hell are you?

—Okay, Eddie says. Okay.

Fritz leads Eddie into the living room. Eddie sits down on a plastic-covered recliner.

—Angela, Fritz calls, c'mere. Grab a couple brewskies.

A middle-aged blonde woman comes in with two cans of beer. She wears a house dress and apron.

—Here's the ball-and-chain, Fritz says. I mean the better half. Just kiddin' you, honey.

Eddie stands up. The plastic chair cover krinkles.

Angela hands him a beer. —Hi.

—Hello, Eddie says, pleased to meet you.

—Ed, here, Fritz says, is an old pal of mine. Comrade in arms, you might put it.

—Oh. Angela turns and goes back to the kitchen.

—Nice home, Eddie calls after her.


They walk after dinner.

—Good for you, Fritz says, patting his beer gut. —Work off a little of this.

Eddie nods and takes the cigar Fritz offers him. Fritz leads Eddie to a small rise and points out the water tower, high school, mall. Eddie looks out over the terrain. He had remembered it as flat, not gently rolling.

Fritz points to a house. —My boy lives there. Down there at the mall, we got some quiet interests down there.

—You really made something of yourself.

—Hell, it could all have been yours. Fritz relights his cigar. Look. Look and you see. I paid my dues.

—And me?

—The past is the past, Fritz says. Nobody wants it back.

—Can't get it back, Eddie says.

—Don't look so pure, Fritz says. There's that thing, that thing you made small, but it's still there. Could come back on you. Unless you do right, you know?

XVII

Fritz has a rec room with a wet bar in the basement, and he throws a drinking party. His boy is there, and Eddie, men from the subdivision, friends from the firm. Eddie sits on a ladder-back barstool, drinking draft from the beermeister. Fritz works the bar in his NAME YOUR POISON apron. Later, they will show adult videos on the wide screen TV. Now a football game is going. Eddie cannot see the screen. Fritz puts a bowl of popcorn in front of him.

A beefy man called the Colonel tells about his days in the firm. The others laugh.

—You remember, Fritz? the Colonel says. Christ, I don't know how we did it. —You remember that one?

—That one and many more, Fritz says. He is drinking gin from a water tumbler, and his face is flushed. —Christ, if we had time to go over all the stunts we pulled. Fritz fills a plastic pitcher from the beermeister and places it in front of Eddie. —Cheer up, sad sack.

Eddie nods weakly.

—Grim one, the Colonel says. What's to be grim about? We're all friends here.

Eddie nods again.

—Trying to bring us down? the Colonel says.

—Easy, Fritz says. How about a fresh drink?

—I'm easy, the Colonel says. Just asking a question. An easy question at that.

—Huh, Eddie says.

—It's not like I'm going to stand him on his head, the Colonel says.

—Our friend, here, suffered a loss, Fritz says. His wife and dog, home and family—

Eddie bends down his head and cries.

—Is he sick? Fritz's boy says.

—Don't, Eddie says, don't ever speak their names again.

—I get you, Fritz says.

—No names, the Colonel says. He's that much sense at least. At first, I wasn't sure.

—How about another, Colonel, Fritz says, another story of the battles we've won.

The Colonel and Fritz laugh. Fritz walks from behind the bar and throws his arm around the Colonel's shoulders.

They sing:

> The damage I've done,
> And the battles I've won,
> The past I'll disclose,
> And the secrets I'll enclose,
> We've had troubles and guns,
> Now the dirty deed's done,
> And my love for you, dear, has just begun.

Fritz goes up on tiptoe for the last line, stumbles. The Colonel catches him. The guests applaud and whistle. Fritz sits on a stool next to Eddie.

—I got a rich one, he says. Tell me, Ed, are you familiar with the boxer in the cage?

Eddie grunts.

The Colonel shakes his head.

—We had this philosophy professor, Fritz says. From a major university, yet. How the hell he ended up in our hands, who knows? This was the old detention center, with cages where the guards walked overhead on catwalks. Foreign design. Called them tiger cages. So the professor goes in the cage. Fat, lazy bastard with spectacles. We figured he'd go nuts without his books. At first it looked that way, but then he started to work out. Shadow box. He'd box and box and run in place and do push ups and so forth, all fucking day, every fucking day. And it worked. Old fatty trimmed down and muscled up, but it affected his mind as well. They call him out of the cage, and he won't budge. Insists he's a fighter. So Stan Leary goes in after him, and sure enough, he breaks Stan's jaw in three places with a left hook.

The Colonel laughs.

Eddie puts his head down on the bar.

—Of course, Fritz says, we had to shoot him.

—How about that movie? the Colonel says.

—Soon enough, Fritz says. We haven't finished the preliminaries. He reaches over the bar and gets a deck of cards. —Little three-hand, eh, boys? He elbows Eddie in the ribs. How about whippin' the old third hand out?

The Colonel sits on the other side of Eddie. Fritz deals each of the men three cards, face down. Eddie tosses off a mug of beer, then another.

—Who was at the house that night? Eddie says.

—Like I know, Fritz says.

—Like anybody knows anything, the Colonel says. He snaps his fingers.

Fritz's boy comes down the bar and refills Fritz's and the Colonel's drinks.

—So I'm psychic, Fritz says.

—A fortuneteller, the Colonel says.

—Shut up and flip over the cards, Eddie says.

Eddie has three queens, each depicted by a nude woman. The queens of hearts and diamonds look familiar. The queen of spades has black tape over her eyes.

—Imported, Fritz says. Scandinavian, get me?

—Turn them up, Eddie says. Turn it fucking over.

—In a nutshell, Fritz says.

The Colonel laughs. —Which one is it under?

—Practice hand, Fritz says. He scoops up the cards. —I'll deal the fair deal of the just.

Eddie lurches toward Fritz.

The Colonel pulls Eddie back. —Sing us a song.

—Gimme a drink, Eddie says.

—Song first, the Colonel says.

Eddie stands on his bar stool and sings:

> Looking out o'er the brim o' me gimme cap,
> I see the world and the sun shining bright.
> It shines through the day and on through the night,
> It burns through my eyes, Lord it's too fucking bright.
> It burns and it burns to the back of my skull,
> And some days I ask myself if I'm doing well.

Eddie sways, changes tunes, and rasps out:

> Drink your whiskey, drink your gin,
> Don't be afraid of anythin',
> Forget the old lady and original sin,
> Down the whiskey, finish the gin.

He clambers down from the stool.

—Wa aah aah, Eddie says. He coughs, doubles over.

The Colonel strikes him sharply on the back. —Quite a performance. Ought to take a prize.

Eddie straightens up, panting.

—What could we award our friend? Fritz says.

The Colonel takes a trucker's wallet from inside his coat. —Damn, I'm a bit short.

—Don't be vulgar, Fritz says. It should be something more personal. What would you like?

—Like? Eddie says. I'd like to be—no, that's stupid.

He takes a gulp of beer.

—No, the Colonel says. Tell us what you want.

—Let it go by, Eddie says.

—Maybe a rubber suit, Fritz says, with a crest on it? A trophy? Loving cup for public display?

—I had it all, Eddie says.

—Have you, now? The Colonel says. Well, pardon our fucking offerings. Obviously, they're trinkets to a man like yourself, a man who knows it all.

—Hey, Fritz shouts, let's put the movie in. Freshen up the drinks, boys. This picture is guaranteed to wet your whistles.

Fritz's boy fiddles with the VCR. The men drag chairs and stools to the TV. Eddie stays at the bar.

—Come along, friend, the Colonel says. This will perk you up. Love, eh? *Amore,* get me?

—Uh huh, Eddie says. He goes behind the bar to fill his pitcher. —I'll be along.

—Pulling that, the Colonel says. I never thought you'd pull that on us. And at a party.

Fritz walks over from the TV. —Come on, fellas. You'll miss the matinée.

—This guy, the Colonel says, is a piece of shit.

—Colonel, Fritz says, I am asking you, please, please, don't start in.

—Got you fooled, huh? the Colonel says. Duped. I can see right through him. Beneath the attitude and the education and the sweet tenor voice is pure shit. And it makes me want to puke all over the room.

—My parts, my title, and my perfect soul shall manifest me rightly, Eddie says.

The Colonel reaches across the bar and grabs a bottle. He swings at Eddie's head, but Fritz steps in front of the Colonel, blocks the bottle, draws a heavy antique pistol from inside his shirt, and cracks the Colonel in the head. The Colonel crumples and falls spread-out on the floor.

Fritz shakes his head. —There used to be three Colonels. Some of you boys take the Colonel to his couch.

—Never seen a pistol like that, Eddie says.

—Chinese, Fritz says. Wanted one for years. Kept the eyes open, and got a hell of a price. I'm a collector, you know.

Eddie gulps his beer. —I'd forgotten there was such a thing. The house, the beautiful objects beautifully displayed, the family. The happy family.

Fritz sits down, bends forward, his face next to Eddie's face. —Lemme tell you something.

—Yeah, Eddie says.

—You went wrong, man. All wrong. Now, how could anybody live like that? Christ, I just can't see it.

—Maybe I belong in a cage, Eddie says.

—I'm not talking about what you did. I mean, it's the betrayal. What did anybody ever do to you?

—I never meant to be wrong, Eddie says.

—You know they're out there. One, two, three. Same thing. Like fucking—like fucking scarecrows on a hill. They can't do nothing, but they're always in the background.

—They're there, I'm here, Eddie says. That's all I got—all I got to go on.

Fritz snaps his fingers. His boy refills his glass. —This world is hard. You get that when you're young. If you got a brain, you know?

—Hard and harder, Eddie says.

Fritz's boy refills the beer pitcher.

—You did wrong, Fritz says, be clear on that. But you did something. Wanted some, got some. Hand it to you there.

—Er, Eddie says.

Fritz's face bulges like a hideous balloon. —They get you. Get you in a room and tell you what you did.

—Join up with me, Eddie says. We'll get others, too.

—What, have you been watching movies?

XVIII

Eddie wakes up. He is flat on his back on the bar, a drink in one hand and a dead cigarette in the other. His trousers are gone, and he is surrounded by burnt-out candles. Eddie sits up. Some of the candles fall.

The rec room is empty. He goes into the bathroom, pisses, looks in the mirror. There are blue lines on his forehead and cheeks. Eddie rubs his face: pool cue chalk. He drinks some water, wanders around the rec room.

A hand sticks out from under one of the couches. Eddie stares: Thick, hairy, veined, a gold band on a finger. He feels dizzy, squats, bracing himself on the edge of the couch. Eddie grabs the hand, yanks.

Fritz glides across the floor. —Wha? He pulls out his pistol and points it at Eddie's face.

Eddie slaps the gun away. —Where are my fucking pants?

Fritz blinks. —Yeah. You checked out.

—My clothes?

—Dead to the world, so we gave you a wake. The boy put that BURY IN A.M. sign on you?

—My pants?

—Hell, they bury you in half a suit. Pants? Somebody put them someplace.

Eddie walks away. He looks behind the bar. Fritz snores. Eddie finds his soiled pants on the VCR. A hole has been burned through the fabric above the right knee.

The house is quiet. Eddie takes a soda from the refrigerator and goes out the back door. His watch is missing.

He sits on the stoop. The sun shines bright. Eddie finds a cigarette in his shirt pocket, lights it, opens the soda. He notices a birdhouse on a pole in the yard. Three stories and a roof shingled with tiny asphalt shingles. Multiple holes. Not one of those order-through-the-mail items. Hand-crafted.

A wave of nausea. Eddie stands up, inhales deeply, tries to

relax, inhales again. He stumbles to the plastic trash can beside the house, lifts the lid, vomits into the can. He vomits again. Eddie straightens up and immediately bends over the can again. The screen door slams.

—You're sick.

Eddie raises his head. It is Angela. —Fine, fine, Eddie says. He lowers his head and retches.

Angela goes inside.

Eddie clears his throat and spits. He wipes his mouth with the back of his hand.

Angela comes out and hands him a mug of tea and a paper napkin. —Maybe this will help.

Fritz comes out. —Heard you were a little under the weather.

Eddie waves the empty mug. —Much better.

—Purged, eh? Best thing. Fritz yawns. That's what these parties are all about. All these guys sitting in their houses, they need to get out and blow off a little.

—I understand, Eddie says.

—Good for the head, Fritz says. For the brain. Veins, too. Massive dose of alcohol cleans out all the cholesterol and plaque. Not every day; that's too much. But once in a while.

Eddie finds a surplus store in the strip mall and buys some multipocketed pants. Used, but durable. He changes in the dressing room, stuffs his old pants in a trash can.

Eddie admires himself in the plate glass of a vacant storefront. Pants look fine, but the hair is a problem.

When the barber finishes clipping, Eddie's hair is cropped near the skull. The barber brushes Eddie's face, steps back to admire his work. —Nice and even, but something's missing. How about a shave?

—Ah, Eddie says.

—On the house.

The lather is warm and moist.

The barber pushes the chair up.

—Finished? Eddie says.

—Almost. He wraps a towel around Eddie's face. The bell over the door rings. Eddie jerks, tries to get up. The barber pushes him back into the chair.

The barber unwraps the towel. A slender young woman stands by the door.

—That's Sally, the barber says. She's buying me out.

Sally waves gently.

The splayed fingers shock Eddie. The hand remains in the air, floating free, although Eddie can clearly see that Sally's hand has returned to her side.

Eddie presses a bill into the barber's hand. —Gotta bolt.

He starts up the hills that lead to Fritz's house. Eddie's breathing is labored. He sweats. His steps are jumpy.

At the top of the first hill, several long, low concrete buildings and a parking lot. Small islands in the center of the lot. The islands are encircled by curbing and covered with grass and trees. Eddie sits under a tree.

He leans against the rough bark, tilts his head back, tries to catch his breath. There is a gentle breeze. Eddie feels the sweat drying on his face. He looks up through the branches. The clouds part. Birds sing. Eddie feels the wind in the trees, the sway of high branches.

If he could, Eddie would stay here, breathing the fresh air. If he could talk to someone, make a deal, get his old job. They could set him up with materials, and he could stay here to capture the light and colors. Eddie can see a sort of purity. A purity he has often heard of in descriptions of places where the earth is pure and the sky is pure and the water is pure, in the pure land.

He gets up and walks, circles the base of the tree. Eddie steps off the curb. He is out of the trees.

Eddie can see the clear sky. He sees Deirdre. He realizes it is not Deirdre in the sky. It is Dolores.

Dolores superimposed on the dome of heaven, not a body or statue, but a stylized, two-dimensional Dolores of crumpled and resmoothed gold foil washed over with blue and white and sepia washes. The sky and sun shine through her. Eddie stands, unable to move.

—Wake up, Fritz says.

Eddie is waiting for something from Dolores. If she will speak. Sometimes it seems her lips are moving a little, but Eddie knows her lips are not moving and that she will not speak to him.

Fritz takes Eddie by the shoulders and shakes him. —Come on.

Eddie waits. For birds. Birds often bring signs.

Fritz has Eddie in a complicated hold. There is a nightstick across Eddie's throat. Fritz pulls. Eddie cannot resist. His eyes are forced downward. He gasps for air.

Fritz gets him in a car. —I don't mind telling you, you had me worried. Christ, what happened to your hair?

—Neat.

—I find you shorn, Fritz says, in those pants, staring at the fucking sky like a fucking turkey in a fucking rainstorm. What the fuck were you looking at up there?

—Long gone, Eddie says. Nothing there.

Eddie falls asleep in the guest room. He wakes when he hears the doorknob turn. A woman stands framed in the lighted doorway.

—Dolores, Eddie says. His eyes fill with tears.

—Are you all right? Angela says.

—Yes, Eddie says. I was dreaming.

Angela turns on the light. She has a tray. —I thought you might be hungry. I brought you soup.

—Thanks, Eddie says. Sorry for all the trouble.

Angela speaks softly. —Fly out of here. As soon as you're strong, get up and go.


—There's the boy, Fritz says. He is drinking coffee at the kitchen table. —Little lady had to go see her family. One of these so-called emergencies. Plenty of cereal or toast. Just have to bach it for a few days.

—I was thinking, Eddie says, I better head out.

—They'll dog your every step. That's no way to go.

—You have another way?

—I have a rec room.

—You got something for me, Fritz, lay it out.

Fritz laughs. —You're like a fish that asks where the fucking water is. He throws Eddie a folded newspaper. —Look through this. I have to make some calls.

Fritz walks out of the room.

—Don't, Eddie says. If I could find the right pattern, then follow it. Do everything exactly right, because if there is one mistake, one little fuck-up, that is it. You have to start over. Try. Try and try. Begin. Start over. This time—

## XIX

Eddie drums slowly on the table with the bundled newspaper.

—Good for something, huh? Fritz says. Let's take a ride. We'll use your auld Olds.

Eddie starts for the driver's side.

Fritz blocks his path. —I know the way.

—Whatever. Eddie settles into the passenger seat.

Fritz tears out of the drive. —I might be able to put you on to something. What I ask is that when you have your look, you see it clear, with a fresh eye.

—I can do that.

—We've always gotten along, Fritz says. He follows a

country road through the woods, swerves onto some ruts, takes the track as it winds down a hill, pulls up next to a black sedan in a dirt lot.

Eddie gets out of the car. A swift river flows near the lot. Tire ruts begin at the far end of the packed dirt and lead to a one-lane wooden bridge. Across the water, there is a clearing and a new, large log house. A screened porch runs around three sides of the house. A stone chimney is built into the remaining side. Little puffs of smoke rise from the chimney. There are utility buildings, a large wood pile, tilled garden, then the low shrubs, brush, woods. A new truck is parked in the driveway. A chow sleeps on the lawn. Deer browse in the forest. Birds sing.

A woman steps out onto the porch.

Dolores.

—You still with us? Fritz says.

Eddie looks. Fritz stands with a man in a dark suit.

—I know you, Eddie says. You're, uh, Businessman—

—Yes, the Businessman says.

—The Businessman of the—the—the—the—

—Whatever, the Businessman says.

—Only forty-five minutes from town, Fritz says. What you wanted? This is it?

—That woman, Eddie says.

—You two be friends, Fritz says, real good friends. After all, we're all human here.

—That's so true, Eddie says. He steps toward the bridge. —I can just, ah . . .

—One thing, Fritz says. Maybe we should dump the shit from the car. You know, clean slate and so forth.

—Absolutely, Eddie says. He steps back to the Olds, opens the trunk, begins taking things out. Fritz gets the stuff from the interior. They waddle, heavily laden, to the bridge and set their piles down. Eddie throws things into the water: fast-food containers, porno magazines, a broken shovel, rags, Bob's forty-five, Jim's nine-millimeter, Mr. Thompson's .357, a sawed-off twelve-gauge, a .308 carbine, a .410 derringer, a boot knife, a twenty-two revolver, a machete, a forty-four single-action, a cash box, an aluminum flashlight, a stun gun, a twenty-gauge double, a cash bag, a thirty-thirty, a click knife, a nine-millimeter short, a styrofoam cooler. Fritz whistles a soft tune. Everything sinks but the cooler. Eddie watches the white box run the swift course for a moment, then turns toward the house.

—One thing, Fritz says. He taps Eddie's chest.

Eddie laughs, takes the twenty-five from his shirt pocket, throws it as far as he can. —Maybe we should dump the car?

—Bad for the environment, Fritz says. Don't worry, I'll bury it for you.

Eddie starts slowly over the bridge.

—I'll walk you across, Fritz says.

He trails behind Eddie, singing sweetly:

> Many's the year I rambled alone,
> O'er plains and mountains, forsaken me home.
> Some think it sufficient to live for the lance,
> But I know a man alone's got no fucking chance.

Eddie steps onto the opposite shore.

They come in a blast. Men in the trees, on the roof, from the porch, the sheds, the woods, all firing guns. Eddie swerves, dodges, turns. He sees flashes. Fritz and the Businessman. Eddie spins in a wheel of fire.

The Businessman yells. —Hurry up, motherfuckers! **Q**

## The City of Portage

The widow did not want to go in the boat. She said so, too, she did. Twice in the rapids, the widow said, that sun too hot, that Peshtigo water chafing her with rust and biting silt—bloat, the widow said, the river up, the boat bark weak.

But the man appeared not to have heard her. He was bailing something puddled out of the hull, spilling it onto the loose earth.

They ought, too, to think of the boy, the widow said.

"Ought what?" the man said.

"Him not half-grown," the widow said, "the Peshtigo drunk, him—the boy—head-over-heels into water, rock, blood," she said. "Bloody, bloody river."

"A story, that," the man said, not stopping bailing.

She would rather not have looked. The man's hands, the widow knew, were rough, the webs of flesh blistered.

"That boy was no account of yours," the man told her. "Don't fill your head. That boy was thick. That boy most likely must have jumped."

The widow squatted down to gunwale level. No, she said, no. She had eyes. She was not so thick herself or dim or gray as all that. So he could save his p's and j's, she said, whatever else, excuses, rancid wet birch lunch, strokes. She had her canvas shoes. She had a widow's intuition, cash. No more questions needed, please, she said. It was decided.

"Can't," the man said.

"Can't?" the widow said.

The man was doing something with the nails of his fingers. She stood.

"Can't get to there by overland alone," the man said.

There was a sound the widow heard and could not place. There was wetness in the bends of her elbows, a low-boiled feeling deep between her breasts. "And what about the burden of portage?" she said.

"Justice," the man said. "Blind."

Then she would steer, the widow said. No questions, please, or boyish sciences of his of navigation. No, sir, the widow said. It was decided.

By talk? he said. By chance? he said. By devil double daring? Would she holler them across? the man said. Take it sheer will or miss? the widow thought she heard him say. By echo, did he say? Had he said echo?

The river's hue was something rare, the widow saw. It was the riverish hue of each rare, raging thing and thing's shadow, each shadowy submergence rising up against the boat. Dark under-paddle Peshtigo, the widow saw, was flush, ored, flushing under her and minerally lit against a widow's washy stroke. No dumb rush, this, the widow saw, no passive mincing brook, this was mineral intelligence, a sparkle like a smart glint of eye, a knower's wink she would as soon have not seen. This was mettle, ire, an unmined bed of metal husbandry below the widow's body. She rocked, she listed, she listened to the rap against the birch, against the rocks, the rapid rising sluice, the rising Peshtigo a hard hue and scratch against a parched-white side, against a hull, against a widow's nettled passage. The man was a foment of foamish motion up in front. He was a mannish birchy sound from a direction she did not wish to steer to, to hear from—down, a wrap-around of blind-dark curve of rapid dark, dark as unbroken day and sucking dark orish rush, a dark crack against a dumb cut of stump, a stand of reed, ragged edges of the overhangs of sere-dark shore, red knolls and rottish woods, soft, swelled, the opened second-sighted flesh of a boy, the mudded dell, the swaddled shores of Mother Leary's shedded unlanterned dark. Leery O'Leary of the unquenched flame, of flamish lullabye and Peshtigoish bedtime tale, the boat a cradle in the rocks, un-

bound, a cradled falling, falling. The corded flesh was singing.
The widow was puckered and crooked and raw—dark Peshtigo
an unseasoned salt against the skin, whetting, sharp, a liq-
uored lick, a trickle tunneling the breasts and chastened nar-
rows of the legs, a puddled hold of natatorial intelligence as
yet not plumbed, a dampened sun, a watered absence sunk
beneath a widow's loose and tendered flesh. She was soaked,
drenched, drained. Undrunk. She was widowed. She did not
wish to rest. She did not want to speak. She did not want to
see to concede to the man, to the boat that she was night-blind
lost, that she was going near to gone.

The Peshtigo was quick.

Was she watching at all? the man wanted to know. The
Peshtigo was not the Kinnickinnic, he said. Was she carrying
a grudge?

"Nicolet," the widow said.

Would she look? the man said. Pay attention to the river?
Was she even half trying to steer, to hold to course?

Need he ask? She could not even swim, the widow said,
much less, nor he—boyish missing Nicolet, the widow said,
and, in fact, she did not want to start.

"Please," the man said. "Not now."

She could see that he was doing something scraping, some
scrapey-sounding thing along a rib of the boat.

"And what of the wife?" the widow said.

"Port," the man said.

This was important.

"Did Nicolet leave a wife?" the widow said. "Was there
one, a water widow? And you?" the widow said. The man's
shirt, she saw, was wetted clear to glistening in back.

Was she deaf? the man said. Could she follow a direction?

Listen. What she was, the widow said, was sore. Her elbows were achy, her knuckles, palms. They were not even

French, the widow said. Nor Sioux. So she was following a hunch and going starboard.

The man had turned to partway face her, but nothing fine was showing in the black of an eye.

"Furry traders," she said.

"Not here," the man said.

"Not even Chippewa," the widow said. "Dunked." But it was harder than not by now to hear him. Did he say rock? Did he say just? Did he say paddle to port? Did she know where she was going, did he say? The widow felt a hewing up beneath her and through her, a succumbing coming up, and the heat of something not completely fathomed. "Father," she said.

Was she crazy? she heard. Rock hull, she thought she heard, straight. But she was pressing through a history herself and said Marquette. They were not even Irish. Oh, Joliet, she tried to say, oh, Father—to hear how the sound of her voice was dissolving, melting, crazed. Fire-watered traitors, the widow tried to utter and could not—not quite. Shawano, Oconto, De Pere, the widow tried. Wauwatosa. Was he shouting, the man, at her? It seemed he was, for he was, after all, a man of his time, another time, another region. Was it Germantown? the widow tried to wonder. The city of Portage? Eau Claire? The man's mouth was of the river, of the Peshtigo—the legend undertold. The widow's tongue-tip tinned. Sheboygan, Superior, the widow tried to say as something in her sight began to cant. She was tilting to an unsung place—to a Peshtigoan dairyland delivered up to flame, a leak of history, a snuffing. O'Leary—this coincidence of consequential loss— oh, Prairie du Chien, she might have whispered. Did Chicago burn as willingly, as well? The widow was rushing through a sibilance of grace, through winded cities—bitter red, ash, bitter, bitter river, bitter shore. She was flicking off retention. Was there fire in the unblooded web of flesh and loin, a bone of knowing? Was there wedding of the elements? Did bottom-living minerals anneal?

This is second-guessing.

For a time, the empty boat would be a telling in itself, the man another christened vessel. And the widow? Oh, widow— she would not not be counted. She would get to there, if only by the broken skin of dreams. For she'd conceived a destination such as this—to be found, to be found not wanting in the current, in the peril, in the rapture of a stream. Q

## ELEANOR ALPER

### *Our Father Which Art in Heaven*

We are finding them, what he is leaving here, these things he is leaving in the night—things we think, or we hope, he is leaving for us—are, or some are, or could be just things which were left over, or else things left which were first left elsewhere, left-handed gloves, or things looking second-hand, hardly hand-picked, even the fruit, picked over, or things he gets for free. We are saying, some of these things left could be things stolen—surely the wood, you would think. Think of where you would buy new wood in the night—his night in the middle of ours, when it is, he gets and he leaves what is left. Some of us are saying they know it for sure where this new wood was, or still is stacked nearby in neat piles there for the taking, the same wood the same ones are saying they themselves were wanting to take—not that they did, but if he did—this wood is somebody else's wood. Not that we need it, this wood or any wood, or most of what is left—so forget about the wood.

What matters that matters, that is, to us, is his leaving us anything. For sometimes for long times there is nothing left except for the paper—one of the free, for-nothing things, he gets, we know, for us for sure. This paper he never forgets to leave feels so soft to touch, it is hard not to hold it up to your cheek. His paper left looks so fine you only want to try to do your best with it. We use his paper to make the things and the cards we leave for him on those days you get and you give cards. We leave him his things on the chair, a dining room one, the only one with arms, and the same chair he is using to leave his shoes under, underneath the rungs, where it is we find nickles and dimes and pennies, those new copper pennies left in the hollows of his shoes, meaning for sure he wants us to shine them.

This is in the morning when we look for and we find, or whoever is first to be up finds what is left—when it is we take tastes of what he leaves: of strawberry ice cream, or of cold smoked eels with skins to peel off and bones to watch out for we fix for our breakfast. If there is nothing left, we look in the trash for any of his stubs or his bills paid, or bills unpaid, crumpled up or torn up too tiny to be put back together—which, after they are, is how it is we find out where he was, with those names that sounded so far away, and what he bought that we never saw, and what he has sold that we thought we had lost. We pick through his pockets for chocolate and Chicklets, and down past his pocket holes into his linings for loose change, where we find at different times and in different holes our missing puzzle pieces, and skate keys and the keys to our locked boxes, and all of his fortunes printed next to his exact weight—which weight we find is getting to be less and less.

The morning we find him—not moving, not really, not even sitting up enough to be sitting on the very same chair he uses to keep his shoes under, wearing shoes still shined-up from our last-time shine—is the morning he is taken away, even before breakfast—when we look up in his attic, which one of us says is sure to be full of what he never left, where his mattress must be stuffed with all of the rest, is where all we find are birds flying and birds eating bird seeds off his bed, and birds fighting for the best spots at a real bird feeder nailed on with far too many nails to a new shelf on the window sill of the window he left open wide enough for the biggest birds, made from what looks like that new wood he left, and not a drop of bird droppings left anywhere here on any of what were our father's things. **Q**

## In the North House

We see boats. Up river from your city is where we live. Sometimes tugs. Sometimes barges loaded full. Sometimes storybook boats hauling their slabs. We know what we are looking for—men on the boats wearing high rubber boots. Our mother wears high-heeled shoes even in winter. Our mother in the kitchen makes tight turns between the stove and sink. Where she goes, go we, Hula-Hoops around our waists. At night we hear her, the click and thuck and clap of heeled slippers on the stairs. Mother says yours is a city of all the hours, that after cargo is unloaded, men walk out into a midnight bright with people and light, where, smelling of diesel and fish, they can peel down their high rubber boots and find a hall where they might dance. Mother says the waltz is a boatmen's dance, it having the wave's dip and crest. When she finds us, she finds us feet and arms and wooly animals down among blankets, pillows bunched, and sheets wrapped for turbans around our heads. Constantinople. We are her Persia. Our night is the pucker and suck of wind through plastic sheeting on windows. Come morning, braids tucked up in shipman caps, we spot for morning boats. We see boats but not a single boatman, not boot, not cap, but the boastful flap of company flags. There are ospreys. We are ready to walk out over the quick-breaking ice to bring him who tumbles overboard from his sleep hammock in to where Mother stirs our cereal. He is not there. The ice thins and groans. The osprey hovers, plunges, breaks water feet first. Our mother calls us down. Calls us her handsome cabin boys. We are girls. Is it true that you have ballrooms where women can go to dance alone?

By noon, we are elbow deep in red dye, dyeing satin from a dead woman's curtains. There will be dresses and vests and even, Mother says, yardage to raise our own wanton flag.

Mother cannot keep a Hula-Hoop up, though she says she has hips enough to balance her litter of young. Mother's house is vase and pillow, sofa and pot, this and that she buys at other women's houses. Shoes. Shoes. Stockings. Hair things. Soon even the washed, thin bed sheets have been dunked. You know what they say, says Mother, how a boatman builds a widow's walk in every port. I guess I think you see silk and satin on every corner, stepping up into buses, going down into trains. Women. Our stained arms, Mother says, are opera gloves. "Go blonde," Mother says, "go black, it hardly matters. Yours truly named you," Mother says, "and that is what counts." What counts for us is Mother's satin, dyed red in a kitchen sink. And arms, hers, ours, stained high and higher. What counts is the low grunt of breaking river ice and us running—double, double, double stairs up—to Mother's bed to sight a barge with letters we have never seen before painted on a gray side. What does not count is a woman dead in a house up river or Mother saying, "Even the best of us gets picked over clean." What counts are boots, the thick rubber tread, the shank, the shaking off, a hallway corner piled knee-high with boots. We do not see a single boatman on the barge. Soft in the middle, Mother's bed is a rolling-in place. We walk the edge. We walk the incline in. Haul on the bowline. Keep to the edge. Look out. We look out. The osprey is a dark angle over her feeding ground. When we come down, we come down one step at a time, heeled, hobbled in shoes too large, bulges from the funny press of someone else's foot, and ready to redden anything, everything that will take the dye. Mother says that our boy-slim hips are blades that—watch out!—will one day kill a man. Shaking, waggling, she cannot keep the bright hoop up. "Hell! Here is all my booty!" Mother says, and she is jigging towards us, leaving our Hula-Hoops in the wake behind her. Mother says in your city men dressed in tuxedos lie on the opera house floor so that they can hear the singing but, "Please," Mother says, "they should never see the singers." The ospreys who feed off our straight of river have nested in these cliffs for all the time I can remember. At night, wool and limb, we are her Persia.

Do you still work the routes?

Sure, okay, yes, we have killed. And not just our winter starved mice or summer's silly bunched slugs lunging the sweet leafy air. There have been captains, shad fishers, sailors, clippermen, even the occasional barge cook up for a breather. Long before they knew what to know, long before they saw her, a bright red wave of skirt on the riverbank, they were spotted from this high place, high on the river cliff. Raised. Sighted. Pop shot.

If necessary—were you able to turn from the curve of her arm? If necessary, we will do so again.

It is now the one long day of February that lasts all the month long. We wear hats. We wear scarves. Our opera gloves are covered over in striped mittens. Mother leads us, picking her way around the drifts that slope off from the window frames. Her heels drill into packed snow. We are her goslings, following, goose-hearted, looking south. Mother says there is one thing sweeter than a clothesline in July, and that, says Mother, is a line hung in the dead of winter. Now nothing, neither man nor fowl, darkening the river sees our satin curtain rigged, hung straight, thickened with water and cold. Mother does not wear a coat. Up here, where the river winds lift and circle, we make snowmen, armed, faces streaked red from where dye has bled down near Mother's feet. We have seen our ospreys perched together on the branches of the dead elm, but now there is only the chickadees' quick cross from the elm to the feeder, the scatter of seed, and Mother saying, "Will you look at this!"

Is it true that there are no mothers in your city but only women in furs going in through heavy doors?

We roll snow bodies uphill to where Mother takes her time—clipping, posing, hooking heels over the drying line—but when we get there, there is only a path of poked snow and from somewhere Mother shouting, "Is this *red* or is this red?" We leave our snowman, headless yet, to go to where we find her squatting at the seam of cliff trees. Mother lists to one side, hangs back from her underclothes, steam rising from where her current bores into snow. There is not a boatman in sight to raise a bottle for our fireship, or to the satin that mother says is bound to blind and run a sailor into rocks. But Mother stays down, haunched, clitted, dress bunched in one hand and the round of ass a day moon risen. Soon enough, not even soon enough, these snowmen will be in the run-off south like all the rest. We do not care if you cannot remember our names. Just call us all together, just take us with you to a dance hall and let us watch you do a waltz.

It is a dangerous time.

We have killed, but we have never found body or bone of a single man. Bones, yes, there have been bones—mouse and cat, the rack and hip of deer we strap on as masks, or the rotted, soft spike of fish backs that kitty carries triumphantly up to Mother's bed. We have found the twiggy bramble of abandoned cliff nest and the twiggy bramble of nest where our osprey lifts herself up from her new ones to come at us, squalling her frenzied cheereek, cheereek, cheereek. We have found bottles, cans, combs, knotted ropes, boots, boot soles, knives, compasses, oars and bullets hove up river, we guess, off more than one slippery deck. But still we have found no men.

Nights in Mother's bed, we wear the compasses strung around our necks, the little red North man in his North house, so that come morning we chart the drift and current of our sleep. We fall asleep to Mother's names—a sailor Bob and a Captain Jack—and wake to hear her, heels and spatula, downstairs. Come morning, wherever the North man has gone—around Cape Horn, through the Greenland Straits—he is back, fixed in his North house as if we have not turned all night.

We have slept too well.

Captain Jack. Captain Kidd. You. She might have gone anywhere . . .

Outside, the dead woman's curtains are sheathed in ice, a corner cut out, and we jump stairs—double, double down—to see, sure enough, Mother is red this morning, strapless and fitted, the satin, a glazed ice over her hips. And what a noise is this mother! Kettle and pan. Cleavage. The hum, the heels, the sizzle, the mutiny. Breakfast is coddled eggs in cups, spinach nests, and soft cheese blankets that Mother says will put some meat on our bones. Breakfast is pancakes stacked and fruit unfrozen from summer's yield. There are muffins and biscuits, bacon strips and split sausage, the buckle of skillet ham. She cannot stop cooking. Mother says by spring one of us, braids pinned under a middy's cap, will be a stowaway, our rosy, cabin-boy cheeks the treat of both captain and captain's wife. Each of us swears she is not going. Each of us swears she is already gone. Slim-hipped boys, we are girls. The morning boats are passing, sounding salutes for the brightly dyed banner of the dead woman's satin. Is it true that the children in your city are alley cats, going down to the docks to feed on spoiled goods? Mother is handing us plates, bone china brought home, she says, from another empty Nancy's house. She is mincing, she is whipping, she is chopping, is grating, is beating. There are soups and casseroles ready for freezing, sandwiches with crusts cut off, cookies in the shape of stars, of ships, a chain of girls in high boots. Roasts, chops, there are patties shaped by Mother, who does not turn from her stove to see if what passes is barge or raft or tug. We practice knots—slip and bow, granny and clove.

She is going somewhere.

. . .

It is almost never now that we see our osprey out hawking over the shallows. Here it is spring, muddy. We see boats plow past, churning up a river brown and thick. The osprey sits her nest. We have no time for Hula-Hoops. We have read in a book on Mother's table that Constantinople is not called Constantinople anymore. We call our mother's bed Her Bed. The plastic sheeting is off the windows. We have read that there is a truer North outside the North man's house. At night, from Her Bed, we can hear the midnight run to your city, the chatter of boatmen ready to step off the river to dry land.

We say Mother is a red sail coming about in the mouth of your harbor. We say Mother is high boots and a jacket, another mate leaning against a column, watching a woman dance. She is a fur coat entering buildings. A tuxedo. Mother is the opera house floor.

If you see her, tell her there has been no flooding, tell her that we have scared off the women who have come looking for a good deal, for a this or a that, for something left behind. If you see her, tell her it is called Istanbul.

Tell her, please, do not come back. **Q**

# STEVE STERN

## Zelik Rifkin and the Tree of Dreams

### THE LOST TRIBE

Even by the infernal standards of the Memphis summers, this one was unnaturally hot. So intense was the swelter in the apartments above the shops on North Main Street that the wallpaper bubbled, the menorah candles melted into shapes like choirs of ghosts. Great blocks of ice dissolved in their tongs to tiny cubes before the iceman in his saturated apron could carry them upstairs. Ceiling fans turned sluggishly if they turned at all, mired in the heaviness of the humid air. Housewives cooked stuffed kishkes on their windowsills and complained that their own kishkes boiled, their brains stewed in the ovens of their claustrophobic abodes.

All day the population of the Pinch—mostly Jews who liked to call themselves a lost tribe, so far were they scattered from the more kosher habitats of their brethren—kept as much as possible to the shade. Wearing ice bags in place of their yarmelkes, they gathered in panting quorums to say prayers invoking rain. In the evenings, they sat in folding chairs outside their shops, fanning themselves till all hours with limp newspapers from which the print had run. Later on, they brought out picnic baskets and cradles, rolled up pallets, and little spirit lamps. Then they took the short walk over to Market Square Park, where they bedded down alfresco for the night.

A relatively barren parcel of land where an auction block for slaves had once stood, Market Square was tucked behind a row of shops on North Main. It was bordered by an ironworks and the red brick pile of the Anshei Sphard Synagogue, and the Neighborhood House, where the greenhorns were taught how to box-step and brush their teeth. As a park, Market Square had only the barest of park-like attributes. There was a dried-up stone fountain and a ramshackle band pavilion, behind whose trellised skirts local lovebirds conducted trysts. There was an enormous old patriarch oak. It was under the broad boughs of the oak, as if wanting shade from the starry firmament itself, that the citizens of the Pinch made their out-door dormitory.

### FRIENDS AND RELATIONS

Famous for his cowardice all along the length and breadth of North Main Street, Zelik Rifkin spied on the other boys at their adventures. Often he went out of his way just to frown in disapproval over the foolhardy risks they took. Walking home from the Market Avenue School, for instance, he sometimes made wide detours in order to pass by their haunts. He spooked about the levee, hiding behind rafts of lumber and cotton bales, or peeked around corners, looking up into a slice of sky between alley walls. Then he was likely to see them, the redoubtable Jakie Epstein and his cronies, hurtling in their daredevil competitions from roof to roof.

Taking a dim but fascinated view of their activities, Zelik kibitzed the pranks they played on unsuspecting citizens. From a safe distance he watched them singeing a cop's moustaches with a well-aimed magnifying glass, or angling with bamboo poles for the *sheitel* wigs of the orthodox wives, or stealing a camera from the pawnshop to take photographs of couples necking under the bandstand, threatening to blackmail them with the evidence.

Sometimes, though it tied his stomach in knots, Zelik was a witness to their shadier exploits. He saw them waltzing the ticket holders in front of the Phoenix Athletic Club for the purpose of deftly picking their pockets, or beating up on trespassing members of the Irish Mackerel Gang in Market Square. Once or twice he was there in the alley behind the Green Owl Cafe, when racketeers dispatched them into *shvartze* precincts with booklets of policy stubs. He saw them receiving the bottles that Lazar the bootlegger handed them out the Green Owl's backdoor.

If ever they caught him at his spying, Jakie and the boys might invite Zelik to join in their operations, confident that the invitation alone would scare him away. "Nu, Rifkin," they shouted, "come and help us roll Charlie No Legs for muggles. Come on already, we'll get *shikkered* blind and jump off the Harahan Bridge."

Flushed from hiding, Zelik would tell them, "Thanks all the same." Then pulling down his golf cap to the bridge of his nose, he'd coax his legs in their baggy knee pants into motion.

He'd duck out of sight, as he did today, and run straight home to his widowed mother.

"It's me, Mama," hailed Zelik upon entering the cramped apartment above Silver's Fruit & Vegetable. He always announced himself as if the remote Mrs. Rifkin, listlessly pumping the treadle of her sewing machine, might take him for somebody else. She might mistake him for one of the dead relations she set such store by, and thus be given a fright. Behind her rose a mound of unstitched jackets and pants like a hill of straw that refused to be spun into gold.

Smiling wanly, more to herself than her son, Mrs. Rifkin kissed the air next to the cheek that Zelik offered.

"I killed a man this morning," he confided, secure in the knowledge that she never heard him. "I robbed the Planters Bank and rubbed out a teller."

"Just so you're careful," replied his mother, absently feeding fabric to the bobbing needle. "Don't climb too high, you won't sink too low. All I ask is that you be careful. Remember, your father, Mr. Avigdor Rifkin, peace on his soul, was struck down in his prime."

From his vague recollection of his father, a herring-gutted garment peddler with a fruity cough, Zelik doubted that the man had ever had a prime.

Pausing a moment in her labor, Mrs. Rifkin looked up to note the date on a calendar hanging from the faded wallpaper. Produced by a company that had created a device called a rational body brace, the calendar was decorated with illustrations of women in harness. "I see that today is your Great Aunt Frieda's Yahrzeit," acknowledged Zelik's mother in a tone of dreamy anticipation. "That means we'll have to go to *shul* after dinner." Sighing wistfully, she tucked a strand of mousy brown hair behind an ear and proceeded with her automatic toil.

For his part, Zelik had no idea who his Great Aunt Frieda was. In fact, most of the relations whose birthdays, anniversaries, and memorial Yahrzeits (mostly Yahrzeits) filled every available date on his mother's calendar were entirely hearsay to him. He and his mama were the only Rifkins, living or dead, that he knew. But in an otherwise shut-in existence, her trips to the synagogue to light candles and say commemorative prayers were Mrs. Rifkin's sole excursions into the world. They were all she looked forward to, and Zelik, with nothing better to do himself, had acquired the habit of tagging along beside her.

Dumping his schoolbooks in the curtained alcove that served for his bedroom, Zelik excused himself. "Goodbye, Mama. I'm running away to join the circus and ride panthers through hoops of flame." As he started downstairs to his afternoon job in Mr. Silver's market, he could hear his mother faintly uttering her cautionary proverb behind him.

Not gifted with an especially enterprising nature, Zelik was a less-than-inspired greengrocer's assistant. It was a negligence abetted by the grocer himself, who worried enough for the both of them, making the market the one place where Zelik was able to relax.

A troubled man with care lines stamped into his brow as with a brand, Mr. Silver was much too busy looking over his shoulder to keep tabs on a daydreaming stockboy. He was a bachelor, the skittish grocer, said to have fled his native Carpathian village in advance of a rumored pogrom. But despite the considerable distance he'd put between himself and the Old Country, Mr. Silver had yet to feel safe from approaching disaster, and often he confused the local gentiles with the hell-raising Cossacks of his youth. His particular fear was of the Ku Klux Klansmen who staged regular mounted parades up Main Street, with both themselves and their horses enshrouded in sheets and visored cowls.

But for all his apprehensions, Mr. Silver was a generous employer, generous beyond Zelik's worth and occasionally his own means.

"You sure you didn't make a mistake?" Zelik had asked upon receiving his first weekly salary; to which the grocer, suddenly prey to a blinking fit in one sad eye, replied, "Maybe you are needing more?" Then he'd thrown in a peck of apricots as a bonus, and enjoined his employee to "Give your mama a *gezunt ahf dein kop* from Leon Silver."

After a while Zelik could take the hint: Mr. Silver's largess was not so much for the benefit of his assistant as for his assistant's mother. It seemed that the grocer was harboring a secret affection for the seamstress, which he was too timid to express through means more direct than his philanthropy.

At the end of the token few hours he put in at the grocery, Zelik went back upstairs for his Hebrew lesson with Mr. Notowitz. To support herself and her son after the death of her husband, Mrs. Rifkin had taken in piecework. But even supplemented by contributions from the Anshei Sphard widows' fund, her labors brought only a pittance, and so she had been forced to take in boarders. The current was Aharon Notowitz, a teacher of Hebrew and therefore just a cut above a common shnorrer. Chronically short of the rent, the moth-eaten Mr. Notowitz had offered to compensate his landlady by giving her son "post-bar mitzvah lessons" free of charge. It was a wholly impractical arrangement that would have added to the boarder's liability, were it not for the windfall profits Zelik had come by since going to work at Silver's Fruit & Veg.

He would find the old teacher in his windowless bedroom lit by a dirty skylight, sunk as usual in a hobbled armchair surrounded by heaps of unshelved books. Formally attired in the gabardine suit he slept in, his beard discolored by ashes and crumbs, eyes like bloodshot fried eggs, Mr. Notowitz seldom got around to actually teaching. Instead he recounted his sorrows. This was fine with Zelik, who'd long since lost the knack of taking religious instruction; it was only as a concession to his mother, who now and then nourished the notion of her son's becoming a rabbi, that he'd agreed to the lessons in the first place. Moreover, a steady diet of Mrs. Rifkin's memorial days, garnished with the threat of Mr. Silver's transplanted Cossacks, had prepared Zelik to appreciate the old *melammed's* complaints. By the time he came to hear them, such heartsick lamentations were for Zelik an acquired taste.

Touting himself as a once-celebrated scholar, descended from the arch-wizard Isaac Luria, Mr. Notowitz had a favorite gripe: he'd lost his faith. "To this *farkokte* country are following us the demons," he liked to repine, removing a finger from his tufted nostrils to examine the pickings. "But God," pointing the finger aloft, "He stays behind."

### PRINCE OF DREAMS

That summer, while secure within his circle of ritual, apprehension, and regret, Zelik found himself more than ever looking beyond. Though he remained true enough to the routine of his days, a restlessness he couldn't account for had seeped into his reluctant bones. He was spending his evenings as always in the company of his mother, going along on her commemorative errands when it was called for. And since school was out, he worked longer hours in the greengrocery; he hung around Mr. Notowitz's rubbish-appointed bedroom. But still he had considerable time on his hands. There were stretches when, lurking aimlessly, Zelik tried to remember what he'd done during previous summers. Then it seemed to him that, every inch his foggy mother's son, he had sleep-walked through the whole of his sixteen years. But if that were the case, he reasoned, to wake up now might be a shock to his system from which he would never recover.

From a furtive vantage, Zelik kept watch on the exploits of

Jakie Epstein and company. He watched them with his typical censure but found it increasingly difficult to turn away.

Though most of the boys had legitimate jobs of their own to attend to—they hawked newspapers, plucked chickens, sold drygoods in their family's shops—they never seemed to let work get in the way of a good time. With school out they found ample opportunities to run wild. They prowled the rooftops and wagonyards crammed with farmers' tin lizzies, the back alleys leading to sordid underworld dens. They challenged the Goat Hills and the Mackerels to baseball in Market Square, games that generally ended in free-for-alls. But mostly they loitered about the cobbles along the levee.

There they sponged dimes from excursion boat passengers in exchange for the false promise of keeping an eye on their motor cars. They shot craps in the shadows of cotton bales with colored roustabouts, who told them stories of blown boilers and wrecked packets, crimes of passion, and floods. Defying the treacherous current (to say nothing of the undertow, the parasites, poisonous snakes, and man-eating garfish with which Zelik had heard the water was rife), they held swimming races across the river to Mud Island. On the far shore they drank gnat's piss and swapped lies with the fishermen, who lived in a shantytown made from old Moxie signs.

They swarmed up the arm of a huge, freight-loading gantry crane and dived off. This stunt in itself would have been sufficiently harebrained, but the Pinch Gang liked to gild the lily. From the crane's dizzy pinnacle they executed backward somersaults and cunning jackknives, sometimes (as in the case of Captain Jakie) wearing blindfolds to heighten the danger. Barely clearing the docked barges, they shouted obscenities and clutched their testicles before hitting the water. In this way they were sure of getting the attention of the girls, who lolled against bollards and floats, pretending not to notice.

When they were done showing off, Jakie and the boys would wander over to where the girls sat sunning themselves.

The clown Augie Blot, wearing only wet underpants and goggles, might shake himself like a dog in their vicinity, prompting universal screams. Hyman Myer might invite Sadie Blen to feel his muscles and, if she complied, press her to let him return the favor. A playful tussling would ensue. But sometimes their tussling wasn't so playful, and Zelik, peeping wide-eyed from behind a packing crate or a parked DeSoto, would draw in a horrified breath.

Once he saw the dim-witted Lieberman twins, Ike and Izzy, yank Rose Padauer's pinafore over her head. While Ike held the upgathered material in a meaty fist, Izzy whipped off his belt and bound the package tight. "Give a look," cried Ike, the more articulate of the two. "We made a flower."

"Yeah," said Augie Blot with sentimentality, "a rose."

The other boys howled, asserting that the change was an improvement, while the girls stomped their feet in angry protest. But shocked as he was, Zelik had to admit that she did indeed look like a flower: a pale yellow one with a pair of kicking, pink-stockinged stems, and frilly white drawers at the blossom's base.

When especially wrought up, Zelik imagined himself, preferably masked, swooping down Douglas Fairbanks-style to rescue the girls from the Pinch Gang's wicked designs. Afterwards, he was ashamed for indulging such dumb fantasies, involving as they did the childish heroics with which he had no patience. Besides, the truth was that the girls were seldom in any real distress. In fact, they usually gave as good as they got, teasing the boys relentlessly. They cast doubts on the Gang's much-vaunted experience of the opposite sex, reducing them to sheepish blushes, then pushing the advantage: "What'sa matter, can't you take it?"

One of the girls, Minnie Alabaster by name, was distinguished for her unmercifulness. Her mouth was a neighborhood scandal, causing general embarrassment whenever she opened it. "Is that a mezuzah in your pocket or are you glad to see me?" was her standard greeting to the boys, after which her conversation was likely to degenerate even further. Her remarks were notorious. Regarding the Lieberman brothers, who were forever digging at themselves, she might inquire with alarm, "You guys got carnivals in your pants, or what?" And when Moe Plesofsky had his head shaved due to an attack of ringworm, she'd thoughtfully observed, "It looks like a *putz*, only smaller." She always had some off-color joke ("Did you hear the one about the *moyl* who made a coin purse out of foreskins? He squeezed it and it turned into a valise") or a fanciful aside concerning the foibles of North Main Street:

"So I'm on the streetcar when I hear Mrs. Ridblatt whisper to her husband, 'Shmuel, your business is open.' And he whispers back, 'Is my salesman in or out?' "

Nobody, not even the otherwise unassailable Jakie Epstein, was spared the sting of her tongue. Wary of it, the boys tended not to cross her, seldom daring to make her the object of their gags. Also, though Zelik had seen no hard evidence, it was generally acknowledged that Minnie was Jakie's girl. This was not so much on account of her formidable tongue as her devilish prettiness—her gimlet-green eyes and puff of ginger hair cropped after the fashion of Clara Bow, her lips like a twittering scarlet butterfly, the pendulum sway of her hips in the pleated skirts that she wore above her dimpled knees. For such attributes it was assumed that nobody but the Gang's intrepid captain should deserve her, though Zelik wondered if anyone had consulted with Minnie herself on this point.

Naturally, he was as intimidated by her bold-as-brass manner as he was by the antics of Jakie and the boys. Minnie's forwardness, scalding his ears, was as much a subject of Zelik's eavesdropping disapproval as the Pinch Gang's hazardous stunts. All in all, he concluded, the youth of North Main Street were playing with fire, and you couldn't blame Zelik Rifkin, who played it safe, if they got burned.

But when he was alone, Zelik found that he continued to think about Minnie. He imagined that her brazen exterior concealed untapped tenderness and fidelity. She had a pure and sympathetic heart that only he, with the well-kept secret of his amorous nature (a secret to himself until now), could detect. And at night, under sweat-soaked sheets, he came to realize a not entirely welcome truth: he had conceived an infatuation for Minnie Alabaster. It was a passion out of keeping with any emotion he'd ever experienced—an immoderate, reckless passion, so lofty in its aspiration that it left him, afraid as he was of heights, a prey to chronic nosebleeds; not to mention the gnawing discontent that kept Zelik lingering a little longer in the neighborhood streets.

He became less furtive in his daily espionage, sometimes dawdling in full view of the other kids. This wasn't so much a function of audacity as imprudence, the result of an overwhelming desire to be nearer to Minnie. Thanks to his short stature and the meager frame that enhanced his semi-invisibility, however, Zelik was regarded as harmless if he was regarded at all. Powerless as he was to stay put, he was thus further encouraged to step out from behind the wardrobe in front of Shafetz's Discount or the wooden Indian next to Levy's Candy Store.

At the very worst, Zelik's proximity to his peers earned him only the usual spurious invitations, the standard verbal abuse. Twitching his leaky nostrils, Augie Blot might begin the chant, "What's that I'm sniffkin?" to which the choral response was, "Must be a Rifkin—peeyoo!" Occasionally even Jakie himself, ordinarily above such banter, couldn't resist taking a shot. *"Vey is mir,"* he might exclaim, popping his gum with a freckled jaw, "it's Zelik the Shiv! Run for your lives!" Then the lot of them would beat it down an alley in stitches.

Sometimes the girls would enter into the ragging, and Minnie Alabaster was often foremost among them. But Zelik had become a glutton for even her most barbed remarks. Once, with her distinctive flair for the dramatic, she'd clutched at a precocious bosom heaving beneath her sailor blouse.

"Come closer," she beckoned the intruder, "Zelik Rifkin, prince of my dreams."

He knew that he ought to feel mortified, she was mocking him shamelessly, but mockery and mortification were second nature to Zelik. What mattered was that she had spoken exclusively to him, and her words—once he'd stripped them of their original context—could be savored in the privacy of his alcove, recalled in such a way as to evoke a sensation that swelled Zelik's shallow breast and surpassed his understanding.

### ACROPHILE

Then came the heat wave that sent the whole of North Main Street to sleep outside in the park. Formerly, during prolonged hot spells, a family might be forced to spend the night on the roof of their building; they would haul up lamps and mattresses until they'd created a kind of poor man's penthouse. But this summer's heat was of a more hellish intensity than the most longtime residents of the Pinch could recall. All day it baked the tenements so that, even in the slightly less oppressive evening air, the rooftops remained scorching to the touch. The soles of shoes might adhere to the simmering tarpaper, arresting movement, leaving you stuck and exposed till the sun rose to bleach your bones. So the families took to the park instead.

Thus far the Rifkins had remained an exception to the late evening exodus, which included even old Mr. Notowitz. Complaining that the foul breath of demons was driving him out of his room, he'd fled the apartment bookless in his filthy suit. (Though not before loosening his necktie and unfastening his collar stud as a statement of how extreme things had become.) Mr. Silver had warned Zelik and anyone else who would listen that the blistering heat was a conspiracy: "It's the Ku Kluxers that they have cooked it up for getting in one spot the Jews. Then by a single swoop they would slaughter them all." But in the end the grocer also succumbed, preferring to be murdered out of doors than suffocated inside.

Zelik supposed that his mother, whose calendar knew no climate, didn't feel the heat so much as the others. She appeared no more languid and done in from her drudgery than usual. As for himself, Zelik felt it, all right, and what was worse, the terrific heat seemed only to further inflame his passion for Minnie. He yearned for her with a desire that grew like a genie let out of a bottle, too large now to ever stuff back in again. It was a longing beyond his control, that despite himself gave him crazy ideas, and would have kept him awake nights regardless of the weather.

Still, Zelik didn't need his mother with her wholesale distrust of nature to list reasons to stay out of the park. Didn't he already have her litany by heart? There were worms in the grass that crept into your liver through your feet, earwigs that crawled into your brain, mosquitoes indistinguishable in their size and thirst for blood from vampire bats. At night rabid animals stalked the perimeter of the Pinch, with now and again a werewolf among them; and never mind the marauding Klansmen promised by Mr. Silver, when the kids from rival neighborhoods were unfriendly enough.

But on this especially torrid night, as he stood in a window mopping his forehead, watching the neighbors strolling toward Market Square, Zelik achieved a restlessness that challenged his legion of fears. Among the strollers he spied Mr. Alabaster, the tinsmith, in a knotted headrag, his broad-beamed wife in a fancy leghorn hat, with their pistol of a daughter sashaying behind them, and what once had been clear and present dangers seemed suddenly no more than superstition.

"Mama," Zelik announced at the door of Mrs. Rifkin's bedroom, "I'm off to join the wild Indians and cut the scalps from my enemies."

"Just be careful, *toteleh*," murmured his mother from her bed. "Chase the wind you nab a devil, stay at home you don't wear out your shoes." Though her voice was much the same waking or sleeping, she nevertheless surprised her son by rolling over to complain about the heat.

In the park the holiday mood of the gathered North Main

Street community confirmed Zelik in his feeling that he didn't belong. He felt as if he'd blundered uninvited into the starlit bedroom of strangers, though he was perfectly·familiar with everyone there. He saw Bluesteins, Taubenblatts, Rosens, Shapiros, Padauers, Dubrovners, Blens—all of them camped out like pashas on throw-cushioned carpets and folding cots, enjoying the after-hours conviviality. They were exchanging gossip and debating local politics, banqueting on cold chicken and assorted *nosherai,* decanting samovars to sip glasses of tea through sugar cubes. By lamplight, the perambulators surrounding them like circled wagons, women changed the diapers of bawling infants. They played mahjongg in upraised sleeping masks while their husbands—in bathrobes, flicking cigars—fanned themselves with their poker hands. Here a voice was heard reciting Scripture, there another naming the constellation of Berenice's Hair. A Victrola with a tuba-sized speaker, blaring a Misha Elman nocturne, vied with the Original Dixieland Jazz Band through the crackling static of a wireless radio. Children ran around in pajamas chasing fireflies, though some already lay curled up on blankets fast asleep.

Even Mr. Silver, while vigilant in his tasselled nightcap, looked sufficiently comfortable where he sat under cover of a lilac bush, nibbling fruit from a paper bag. And Mr. Notowitz, wrapped in newspapers like a fish but recognizable from his gartered ankles and volcanic snores, was the picture of one who'd slept on stone benches all his life. Meanwhile, having strayed from their family bivouacs, young people were clustered among the roots at the foot of the patriarch oak. The boys rough-housed and scratched initials on the bricks that filled the hollow of the tree trunk like a walled-up door. The girls turned their backs and conspired in whispers.

As he sidled to within earshot, Zelik could hear Augie Blot proposing a contest to see which of the Lieberman twins was the dumber. "Okay, Izzy, first question: Are you Izzy or Ike?" Jakie Epstein was leaning against the tree trunk with folded arms, looking as if the whole proceedings depended on the grace of his lanky, sandy-haired presence. From her giggling confab with Sadie Blen and Rose Padauer, Minnie Alabaster turned on a dare to the silent ringleader: "Hey, Jakie, you still dating that *shikse*, what's her name, Mary Fivefingers?" Some of the neighbors in Zelik's vicinity commented in exasperation over the *pisk* on that Alabaster girl.

Then Augie went into his nose-twitching routine. "What's that I'm smellik?" he called out once or twice before he'd elicited a halfhearted chorus from a couple of the boys: "Must be Zelik." "Rifkin, man of the hour," greeted Augie, showing teeth like blasted hoardings. "Jakie, wasn't you just saying how we needed Rifkin to complete our *minyan*?"

Jakie frowned his irritation at Augie's putting words in his mouth, especially concerning so uninteresting a subject. But then there was always the chance that, under Augie's instigation, something interesting might develop.

Zelik knew it was time to back off and dissolve into shadows, but in the moment that he hesitated (a moth drawn to Minnie's flame), the Liebermans took hold of his arms. They ushered him forward and planted him directly in front of Jakie, who took his measure with a dispassionate gaze that made him shrink. He shrank further from his acute awareness that Minnie was looking on with a sardonic grin.

Man of action though he was, Jakie condescended to speech when his office obliged. "You see, Rifkin," he began with a pop of the jaw, "we got this problem. Seems there's this, . . ." leaving the problem for Augie to define.

"This kite," supplied Augie, pointing straight up.

"There's this kite," continued Jakie, "which it is stuck in the top of the tree—ain't that right, Augie? And ain't none of us got the *beytsim* [Augie, acting as interpreter, clutched himself between the legs] to climb up and fetch it down."

At this Zelik began to struggle against his detainers to no effect. While Augie assured everyone what a lucky break it was that Fearless Rifkin had happened along, the Liebermans hoisted their captive onto the bottommost branch of the oak.

When he tried to scramble down, their arms prevented him, shoving him back onto his swaying perch. Augie Blot struck a match and waved it under his shoe soles until Zelik also had to draw up his dangling feet.

"Now don't he look natural, Jakie," said Augie, stepping back to feign admiration. "A regular Tarzansky, wouldn't you say? He's hugging that branch like I think he must be in love."

"Yeah," concurred Jakie, known to sometimes wax philosophical. "Rifkin wasn't never at home on the earth."

Clinging to his knotty tree limb in a panic, Zelik pleaded, "Have a heart!" He appealed to the neighbors in the grass beyond the serpentine roots, and was told to pipe down, they were trying to sleep. Besides, since he was less than six feet from the ground, those who noticed were more inclined to see humor than danger in his situation.

"Help!" he cried to universal laughter and taunts, one of which resonated in his ears more than the rest.

"Don't worry, Zelik. If you start to fall, you can hang on to your mama's apron strings—which he also uses for tefillin; I got this on good authority."

It was Minnie Alabaster, in whose voice Zelik could take no comfort now. He saw himself, through her eyes, for the pathetic, cowering creature he was, and again in a single night his fears had met their match, overcome this time not by restlessness but shame. And shame, like restlessness, shook you into action. It made you want so badly to distance yourself from the insults hurled from below that, unable to descend, you had no choice but to start climbing.

With a painful deliberateness, his groping made all the clumsier for the racing heart that hastened his ascent, Zelik hauled himself aloft. At every stage he paused to catch his breath, embracing boughs hatched with crude hieroglyphics, taking note of a new dimension of things to be scared of. There were enormous ants and weevils scurrying along the rope-veined branches like scorpions, warts like eyeballs on spatulate leaves. An unseen owl hooted nearby and Zelik froze, snuffling back tears, wiping his nose, which had begun to bleed. Then a fresh round of abuse spurred him into motion again.

Somewhere during his vertical crawl, far beyond the point where he could see the ground anymore, Zelik realized that the taunts had actually turned to encouragement. Jakie's gang were calling him Shipwreck Zelik after the famous flagpole sitter, saluting him for the way he'd risen to the occasion. That's when, rather than cheered, Zelik was struck by the magnitude of what he'd done, the impossible height he'd attained, and he held fast with all his might to the tree.

Afraid to look down, he squeezed his eyes shut but was afraid of the darkness behind his closed lids. So he opened his eyes and looked up. Just above his head was what appeared to be a cobweb shaped in a spiral like a miniature galaxy. Or could it be in fact the ravelled tail of a kite caught in the topmost fork of the oak? His cowardice still screwed to the sticking point, Zelik didn't even dare to reach for it. Instead he clung tighter to the slender bough that nodded with his weight, its bark smooth and unscored by anyone who might have been there before him.

"Attaboy, Zelik!" they shouted; "Rifkin at the roof of the world!" their fickle turn-around galling him even more than their contempt. But while he'd climbed as high as he could manage on the strength of his shame, the wish to get further from their voices gave him one last boost, and Zelik rose another foot or two into the breezy air.

His head had penetrated the cobweb, which turned out to be nothing more than a patch of fog. It cooled his brain, stilled his heart, and left him with eyes wide open, but what Zelik saw made no earthly sense. He was after all in the top of a tree, a fact miraculous enough in itself. But what he seemed to be looking at, from the level of the pavement no less, was North Main Street—the shops and the firehouse, the tenement flats, the movie theater, the cigar factory, the trolley car lines. It was the same shabby street he lived on, its alleys rank with weeds and wistaria, the cooking odors mingling with the stench of the river and the horse poop of mounted police, though here and there some telling detail suggested a difference.

For one thing there was a moon, a crescent like a silver fishtail, where previously the night had been moonless, and its light was strong as sunlight, if softer, and grainy like a fine yellow mist. The buildings looked mostly the same in their uniform need for repair, though the paint-chipped facades were relieved in some instances by an odd architectural flourish: the laceworked wrought iron balcony, entwined in orchids, jutting from the Widow Teitelbaum's window; the giant bare-chested caryatids, which seemed to be breathing, holding up the cornice on either side of Tailor Schloss's door. Projecting from the chimney of a tiny frame house, where a family of *shvartzes* lived beside Blockman's junkyard, was a tall mast complete with yardarms and a billowing blood-red sail. While the shops were identical to those on the terrestrial street, there were certain items out of keeping with the standard merchandise: the golden ram's horn and the pair of magnificent ivory wings, for instance, among the tarnished brass watches and battered ukeleles in the window of Uncle Sam's Pawn; a manikin decked out in the naughtiest Parisian lingerie and an eye-catching coat of many colors among the racks of irregulars in front of Shapiro's Ready-Made. Through the windows of the Main Street trolley, whose tracks passed not three feet from Zelik's head, he could make out an interior as opulent as a club car on the Twentieth Century Limited.

The neighbors were going about their more or less ordinary business, despite random intrusions of the extraordinary. Mr. Sacharin rolled a herring barrel backwards down a ramp from a delivery truck; Mr. Krivetcher arranged his show shelf of only left shoes. Mr. Dreyfus, at a workbench in his shop window, polished a pearl the size of a swami's crystal ball. Max Taubenblatt, in the window of his haberdashery, wearing the hat and tails of a stage magician, prepared to saw his talky wife in half; while next door Lipman the asthmatic cobbler, in lion skins, collapsed the doorposts of his building with a mighty shrug. On a corner Itzhik Bashrig, the *luftmensch*, holding his pail under a faucet, coaxed a pinging shekel from the tap with every flick of his wrist. A woman rode past on Blockman's swayback horse, her naked body concealed by her Godiva hair. The thick blonde tresses were parted in back over a prominent dowager's hump that identified her as Mrs. Blockman herself, the pious junkman's wife.

There was a moment when Zelik wondered if he could have reached heaven. But the monkeyshines of his neighbors were not altogether of the type he associated with a kosher idea of heaven. Besides, so far as he knew, none of these people were dead as yet. Having made this assumption, however, Zelik figured he ought to confirm it, and immediately thrust his head back under the quiet whirlpool of fog. He looked down through the web of branches at the sleeping neighborhood spread out around the base of the tree. Then it occurred to him: what sleepers did was dream. And dreams, one might suppose, rose like heat until they found their common level. There they might settle at a height where some dauntless climber, provided he had the means of ascent, could reach them. He could enter the community of dreams and witness the high jinks to his heart's delight.

But as he looked down, Zelik lost the sense of rapture he'd had only moments ago, and with it he very nearly lost his balance. Reminded that he was still, God forbid, umpteen feet above the earth (where dawn was already breaking), Zelik's fear of heights reasserted itself with a nauseating rush. Desperate, he clung to the oak for dear life.

Once the nebbish had climbed out of sight and shown no signs of coming down, the Pinch Gang began to lose interest. Augie Blot started torturing a bullfrog, pretending to read the future in its entrails, which were ultimately used to terrorize the girls. Eventually, grown bored and sleepy, they'd all wandered off to join their families. In the morning, reassembled at the foot of the oak, yawning and dishevelled from a night under the stars, the remnants of last night's party remembered Zelik. Since the leaves were too thick to determine if he was still dangling somewhere above, Augie Blot was for calling the fire department, while Jakie dispatched his nimbler lieutenants to investigate.

When they saw him being lowered through the branches from which he'd been pried, they marvelled that he'd stuck it out overnight. Moe Plesofsky and some of the others proposed that Rifkin be made an honorary Gang member on the spot. Such fanatical endurance surely entitled him to waive the trials by fire, water, and theft that constituted a traditional initiation. But on closer inspection, when he'd been dropped to the ground in a limp but still quivering heap, they thought better of their benevolent impulses. All of a sudden it was clear that, regardless of what may have compelled him up the tree in the first place, it was fear that had kept Zelik aloft.

"Jellyfish Rifkin," jeered Augie, stepping over to lift one of Zelik's scrawny arms, "the winner and still champeen coward of North Main Street!" Several others joined in the derision, but ramrod Jakie Epstein advised them to button their lips. "He ain't worth the wasted breath," Jakie added quickly, lest they mistake him for a defender of the underdog.

Some of the neighbors, pulling up suspender straps and massaging sore spines as they passed on the way to their homes, did double takes at the sight of the pitiful Rifkin kid. They gazed at him as if, though familiar, he was a stranger whose face they'd seen somewhere before. Among the passersby were the Alabasters, with their tousle-headed daughter in tow. Getting a load of Zelik, she gave him a flirtatious wink, then screwed up her face like she didn't know what had gotten into her.

For his part, Zelik—caked in bird droppings, cap and plusfours hung with twigs—wondered if he were still in a dream.

SHEDDING SKIN

Trudging home in the already hothouse sunshine, Zelik found his mother, who'd yet to miss him, dragging around the kitchen in her dowdy dressing gown. She was setting the breakfast table with typical burnt offerings.

"Today's the anniversary," she announced with an enervated reverence, "of your great grandma, the Bubbe Bobke's passing, who died of what they died of in those days. So after supper you'll come with me to *shul*?"

"Mama," confessed Zelik, presenting the bedraggled spectacle of himself as evidence, "I spent the night in a tree."

"As long as you were careful, my *yingele*. If you climb a ladder, count every rung. You know, your father . . ."

Not that Zelik needed any reminding about the perils that awaited him abroad. Hadn't last night's adventure been lesson enough, leaving him more than ever a bundle of nerves? Should someone say boo, he'd have clung to his mama's bristly ankles and pulled her gown over his head. So jangled was he this morning that he could scarcely recollect how, for a while in the crown of an oak tree, he'd been brave.

But as the day progressed and Zelik went through his perfunctory paces in Mr. Silver's market—grinding coffee, weighing cantaloupes, shucking corn to the weary rhythm of she-loves-me, she-loves-me-not—he began to recall with more clarity what he'd seen from the top of the tree. Or rather, the memory overtook his brain despite his best efforts to resist it. The exhilaration of the previous night returned, dispelling his nervousness, infecting his tepid bloodstream till his insides ran with rapids and cascades. In the end, Zelik's vision of a cockeyed North Main Street eclipsed even his hopeless mooning over Minnie, and he longed to see that ethereal place again more than he longed to see her.

Later that afternoon in Mr. Notowitz's bedroom, as his teacher belched whitefish and remembered past glories, Zelik thought he knew precisely what the old man was talking about.

There was the part, for instance, where, wiping his face with the fringe of his flyblown beard, the teacher brooded:

"Once the Tree of Life I have climbed and plucked the sacred citron—I, Aharon Notowitz, that knew personally what are calling the wise men a holy influx. This by the heart and yea even in the pants I am knowing, when I would wear the garment of light that it was custom-tailored . . ."

"I know just what you mean," put in Zelik from the edge of his chair.

"You?" said the teacher, his blood-rimmed yellow eyes coming to rest on his student for possibly the first time in their acquaintance. *"Pishteppel,* what do you know?"

As the concept was brand new to him, Zelik had to grope for the words. "It's like . . . being awake in your dreams."

"Dreams, shmeams," grumbled the old man, though Zelik thought his sourness lacked conviction. *"Kholem iz nit gelebt,* dreamed ain't lived."

Zelik looked forward eagerly to accompanying his mother to the synagogue that evening, if only for the time it would kill. Absorbed as he was in his anticipation, however, he couldn't help noticing that, despite the ever-oppressive heat, Mrs. Rifkin looked a touch livelier than usual. The indications consisted in nothing more than a slightly diminished slouch to her walk, a clean frock, a hint of rouge, a head-hugging flapper chapeau. But they were enough to make her son question whether the exuberance he could hardly suppress was somehow contagious.

Since sundown came so late during the summer months, the service on this *Shabbos* evening didn't begin till after nine o'clock. It was ordinarily a lengthy affair, with many of the more prominent North Main Street citizens called to the Haftorah readings. Leaving their seats by the eastern wall, these men, often dressed as if for the links, would whisper in the sexton's ear before ascending the bima; then the sexton would relate in a booming voice their contributions to the synagogue building fund. But tonight the service was cut short on account of the general asphyxiation. After Cantor Abrams had lifted his megaphone for a show-stopping *"Avenu Malkenu,"* Rabbi Fein rose puffing in his bowler to make an announcement: The ladies of Hadassah would be on hand with provisions for those who elected to stay the night in Market Square.

To Zelik's astonishment his mama, who as a rule never ventured further from home than the *shul,* heaved a sigh and submitted fatalistically, "Who knows, maybe it'll do us good. Coming, *kepeleh?"*

In the park Mrs. Rifkin set about her mechanical house-keeping as if she were accustomed to sleeping out of doors. Choosing a spot on the edge of the crowd—somewhat du-plicating the apartment's floorplan in its vicinity to Mr. Noto-witz on his bench—she spread the horse blanket dispensed by the Hadassah. She kicked off her shoes, removed her costume jewelry, and took a Yahrzeit candle from her purse. Zelik won-dered why he expected that the candle would be lit.

Nearby under the lilac, Mr. Silver sat nibbling fruit. Upon seeing the Rifkins, he rose and shuffled over, removing his sleeping cap. Zelik waited for him to warn them of impending disaster, but instead he only offered some of his prunes. "Very good on my ulcer, they told me, and for the voiding of the bowel," he assured them, risking an experimental smile at Mrs. Rifkin. It was as close to a declaration of affection as Zelik had ever known him to make. Something, it seemed, was in the air.

Zelik stuck close to his mother, who, after muttering pray-ers and laying her head beside the flickering candle, surprised him again by the ease with which she fell asleep. Once asleep, however, she was her old self again, moaning in the way that distinguished her troubled slumber. From where he sat in parched grass that still retained the heat of the day, Zelik could just make out the other kids under the tree. He strained for a glimpse of Minnie but felt no special disappointment when he couldn't see her. Instead he was content to lean back against the pillow of his wadded sack coat, listening to the A&P Gypsies drowning in a surf of static, the laughter of his neighbors growing spotty before subsiding into yawns.

The hour was late and he too ought to be dog-weary, having had not one wink of sleep the night before, but tired was the last thing that Zelik felt. Warily he got to his feet, beginning to creep about the margins of his neighbors' encampments, picking his way toward the base of the oak. He looked here and there amid the lumbermill of snoring to make certain that no one was watching, then jumped up to grab hold of an overhanging limb.

"I don't do this," Zelik reminded himself as he clambered for a foothold. "Zelik Rifkin doesn't climb trees." So who was it clutching that knot shaped like an old man's grimace, who fending off the flapping of an angry bird whose nest he'd nudged with his head? This is not to say that the dread of almost everything, by which Zelik identified himself, wasn't perfectly alive and well in his system. But tonight anxiety didn't rattle his nerves so much as strum them, tuning them to musical vibrations as he climbed into the cooler air.

In the giddy branches at the top of the tree, without hesitating, Zelik stuck his head through the spiral ceiling of fog. Again he was presented with the street of dreams. Citizens passing by on foot or in automobiles waved cordial salutations to Zelik's disembodied head. Blind Eli Rosen sounded an aooga horn as he rounded the corner in a block-long, articulated touring car; Miss Bialy of the Neighborhood House fluttered her hankie from the window of a solid glass four-in-hand. Filling his lungs with the fumes and aromas that were a tonic to him now, Zelik exchanged his grip on the oak for a hold of the pavement. He pulled himself up, scrambling from what turned out to be a manhole, its cover lying to one side like a huge plug nickel.

He stood in the middle of the street, poised to investigate, when he was struck by a mildly disturbing thought: What if, just as this morning he'd nearly forgotten last night, in wandering away from the manhole he forgot where he'd come from? To refresh himself with regard to his bearings, Zelik dropped to his knees and poked his head back into the hole. What he saw under the fog was a skinny kid in golf cap and baggy knee pants, hugging the wavering branches of a tree.

"This is me," Zelik surmised, curiously inspecting the flesh and bones out of which he seemed to have climbed. It troubled him a bit that his abandoned self should have reverted to so terror-stricken an attitude. Feeling, nonetheless, quite corporeal from his loftier vantage, fully clothed and ready for a little fun, Zelik withdrew his head from the fog as if he'd kept it under water too long. Then, with another breath, he took another look: still there. Again he raised his head, gave a shrug, then got to his feet and set off to explore.

He began with the Idle Hour Cinema, where, as a regular feature of the Amateur Night Venue, the little Elster girl was winding up a tap dance in blackface and bubble eyes. Following her, the manager, Mr. Forbitz, announced, "For your special delectation, . . ." drawing a curtain to reveal Tamkin, the cobbler's apprentice, immersed in an outsize fishbowl, a knife in his teeth, wrestling a large man-eating reptile with a thrashing tail. At the Phoenix Athletic Club they were dragging Eddie Kid Katz, the local palooka, out of the ring, after which the cadaverous Galitzianer rebbe entered in satin trunks. Coached from a corner by a party resembling Benny Leonard himself, he delivered a sucker punch to the apparently glass jaw of a giant wearing biblical sandals and a ribbon-braided beard. From a dolphin's-head spigot on the marble fountain in his candy store, Mr. Levy filled a glass with sparkling liquid, levitating as he sipped it several inches above the sawdusted floor. In his butcher shop, Old Man Dubrovner, tiptoeing into the meat locker, parted hanging slabs of beef to behold what looked like the Queen of Sheba, suspended in a block of ice.

Zelik took in everything with the peculiar wisdom with which he felt himself newly endowed. He understood, for instance, that, while most of these prodigies were authored by individuals, there were some involving two or more dreamers at once. This could, of course, be explained by the fact that the neighborhood slept together, and their dreams were therefore likely to mingle and converge. It was a condition that sometimes made it hard to determine where one person's dream left off and another's began.

Such was the case in the *mikveh* where the Rubenesque Mrs. Kipper, her lower anatomy that of a glittering goldfish, was performing a solitary water ballet, while Mr. Shafetz of Shafetz's Discount looked on indulgently in his fez, blowing words of love in the smoke from a nargileh pipe. It was the case with the Pinch Gang, who were everywhere, performing stunts compared to which their daylight exploits were sissy stuff. They danced without nets on crisscrossed clotheslines strung high across the alleys. At the river they commandeered the sumptuous barge of the Cotton Carnival royalty, dallying with the maids of honor after forcing their escorts to walk the plank.

Returning their greetings, Zelik heartily applauded their reckless abandon. He felt that, while only a spectator, he somehow as good as participated in their mischief. In fact, it occurred to him that being wide awake gave one a sort of edge over the dreamers. You had the power, should you want to use it, to interfere with or even alter the course of their dreams.

But why would you want to do that when everyone already appeared to be having such a good time? Or rather, almost everyone—because, across the street at Silver's Fruit & Veg, the harried proprietor cringed behind his cash register with his apron over his head. A posse of mounted Ku Klux Klansmen, wearing cowls that bore the insignia of the Black Hundred and brandishing Cossack sabers, had ridden roughshod into the grocery. They were dangling a thick noose from a light fixture, threatening to stretch the grocer's Jew neck.

"We gon' do you like they done that'ere Leo Franko down Atlanta-ways."

Nor was everything hunky-dory in the apartment over the market. Mrs. Rifkin was as usual at her sewing, but back in his stifling bedroom Mr. Notowitz was beleaguered by giggling demons. Shaggy little creatures with beaks and crumpled horns, with goat shanks and barbed tails that struck sparks from whatever they touched, were tearing pages from his sacred texts and tossing them gleefully into the air. Bleating depravity, they tugged at his soup-stained beard and knotted the wisps of his hair, while the old man asked the Lord why he'd been singled out for such a distinction. And when he looked again, Zelik saw how his mother, idle behind her antiquated Singer, was staring in dumbstruck confusion at the calendar on the wall. She was studying the glaringly empty square of a single vacant day wherein there was nothing at all to commemorate.

An old hand at nightmare himself, Zelik certainly knew them when he saw them, and so backed away from the situations of his mother and friends. It wasn't that he was frightened; nothing here seemed to frighten him, which was the point. All of a sudden, Zelik missed his native jumpiness, the nerves that set off alarms throughout his body. Light-footed, he missed the lumpish body in which he'd never felt much at home. Maybe, he thought, it was time to go and check on himself in the tree.

Making one last scenic loop on the way, he passed by the Anshei Sphard *shul,* through whose portals he saw dreams that had not so much merged as collided. Inside, Minnie Alabaster was being manhandled, dragged kicking and screaming down the aisle by the Lieberman twins. In a gown of white chiffon and a veil sent flying from her tossing ginger hair, she shouted oaths that caused even Jakie's goons to turn crimson about their jug ears. On the altar stood Captain Jakie himself, looking a little chafed in his top hat and cutaway, with his best man Augie Blot beside him in snazzy pinstripes, a pistol trained on the frowning Rabbi Fein.

In the door of the synagogue, Zelik had reached the conclusion that, given such complicated circumstances, you could hardly apportion blame, when Minnie twisted in her struggle to cry out to him, "Shmuck, you got lead for bones or what?"

At that moment, having wrestled her up the stairs to the canopy, the Liebermans hoisted her wedding dress and bound it tightly over her head. They held her pinned in place but still kicking as the rabbi began dolefully to read the marriage vows.

Satisfied that all was not only big fun in this quarter, that one person's dream might be another's nightmare, Zelik turned and retreated to his manhole. He dropped back into his vacated skin, which welcomed him like a warm bath of worry and fear.

### IN WHICH ZELIK HAS AN AGENDA

With the ounce of residual chutzpah still left to him, Zelik managed a slow descent on his own steam, reaching the ground just in time for sunrise. Where yesterday his muscles had smarted exquisitely, unaccustomed as they were to strenuous exercise, today he hurt in his very bones, not to mention his head, his heart. All that afternoon in Mr. Silver's market he groaned aloud with every least effort, until the grocer was moved to say, "You don't look so good already. Have a sit." No martyr to his condition, Zelik wanted to tell his employer, unusually spruce of late in a rakish straw boater, what he knew no one would believe. In fact, but for the souvenir of his general aches and pains, Zelik was no longer so sure what he believed himself.

"Maybe I overdid it in this heat," he agreed with Mr. Silver, and sat down.

Later on he swapped complaints tit for tat with Mr. Notowitz, griping about the unpleasant consequences of slipping in and out of one's own skin, but fell into a self-conscious silence when he had the impression that the old man was listening for a change. He was irked by his mother's unbecoming friskiness that evening, her air of expectancy. Why should she be in such an all-fired hurry to get to Market Square, where all she did, after a brief chat with Mr. Silver, was lie down and sink abruptly into fitful sleep?

As it turned out, Mrs. Rifkin wasn't the only one bent on

retiring early. All around the neighbors stretched ostentatiously, excusing themselves from bridge circles and checkers, plumping pillows as if they couldn't wait to commence the business of dreaming. Not a bad idea, thought Zelik, who'd had no rest for two nights running, but he was still too keyed up and racked with pain to relax. Unable to get comfortable, he rose, feeling that despite wide-open eyes he was walking in his sleep, limping resistlessly toward the oak. He was in no shape to even consider climbing, which thank you but he'd had quite enough of in any case. Though didn't the conventional wisdom have it that more of what brought on the affliction was sometimes the best remedy?

At the top of the tree, hoisting himself with an excruciating effort into the dreamscape of North Main, Zelik was buoyant and light-headed once again. What's more, he found himself in possession of a program. Making straight for the greengrocery, where Mr. Silver's recurrent nightmare was still in progress, he leapt adroitly astride the haunch of one of the horses, unseating its hooded rider with a shove while retaining his sword. He spurred the spirited Arabian into the market, laying about with his blade, snatching up the terrified grocer whom he folded over the horse's flying mane. The Klansmen reared and spat curses in the name of the Exalted Kleagle before beating a frustrated retreat. Leaving Mr. Silver seated now upon the charger, proudly erect as if posing for an equestrian portrait, Zelik dismounted and picked up a Klanman's fallen hood. He took a grease pencil from the checkout counter, scrawled a Mogen David above the peepholes, and pulled the linen cowl over his head—a wizard's hat.

He shot upstairs past his wilted mama, saying, "Don't go away!" then burst into the room where Mr. Notowitz was suffering from demons. "It is I, your hallowed ancestor, Isaac Luria," he announced, "scourge of goblins and fiends." He took up a book at random from the gutted pile on the floor. "And this is the Book of Raziel that the angels gave to Adam, which he lost like a klutz when he got kicked out of the Garden.

It's the book that answers the question how to look on the Almighty without you should go crazy or blind." He licked a finger, fanned the pages, gave a satisfied nod, and addressed the assembled evil spirits by name:

"Igrat, Pirpik, Qatzefoni, Asherlutz, Hormin son of Lilith, Mahalath

  ahalath

   halath

    alath

     lath

      ath

       th

        h, enough already! *Shoyn genug!*"

Whining that they'd been dealt with unfairly, calling Zelik a spoilsport and worse, the demons began to vanish from their hooves and chicken feet to their spiky, cyclopean heads. To the tune of his old teacher's blubbering gratitude, Zelik made his exit and doffed the hood. He marched past his mother, who was mired in fabric, and stepped up to her calendar, writing boldly with his marker in the single vacant square (whose date was incidentally the present day): RACHEL RIFKIN'S COMING OUT. Then, gently, he raised her from the sewing machine and led her out of the cramped apartment down into the enchanted street. There Mr. Silver, saying "Hi, ho, Leon Silver!" invited her to take a ride on his milk-white steed.

After that Zelik might have rested. On earth he would have rested, tuckered out from the sheer exertion of having imagined such events. But here one thing led to another, the momentum building, carrying him forward as on the crest of a wave that crashed at the threshold of the Anshei Sphard *shul*. Entering, Zelik plucked the cantor's megaphone from its wall sconce, thinking it might come in handy. He stole into the women's gallery to better survey the scene on the altar, still in full swing, the hostage rabbi still pronouncing nuptials over a battling bride. Zelik tapped his temple until a strategy revealed itself. He untied from the railing a rope attached to the Everlasting Light, which in turn hung suspended from a rafter over the *chuppah,* directly above the head of the gun-toting Augie Blot. Then he let go, allowing the lamp, like a small red meteor, to drop through the canopy where it flattened Augie's yarmelke. As Augie crumpled, Zelik broadcasted through the booming megaphone, "It's the voice of the Lord here. Now cut the hanky-panky."

Exchanging fearful glances, the knuckleheaded Liebermans unhanded their captive and bolted, tumbling over each other in their efforts to be first down the aisle and out the doors. Meanwhile, Jakie Epstein, ferocious when provoked, had taken up the fallen Augie's pistol, pointing it left and right. "What's that I'm sniffkin!" he called out, proving it wasn't so easy to pull the wool over his eyes even in dreams.

Welcoming the challenge, Zelik mounted the railing, the rope that held the counterweight of the lamp still in his hands. He swung down from the gallery in a sweeping pendulum arc, neatly kicking the gun out of Jakie's grasp and catching it on the upswing in midair. Then he dropped to the altar and aimed the gun at Jakie, who raised his arms in defeat, muttering as he retired that they would see who had the final laugh. Nevertheless, Zelik thought he'd detected a trace of the ringleader's smile, as if Jakie were pleased at long last to have a worthy adversary. Tossing the pistol, Zelik unfastened the knot that bound Minnie's dress over her head, and stepped back to watch the lace and chiffon fall like petals unfolding. As they faced each other—Minnie drinking in an adoring Zelik with quizzical jade-green eyes—the rabbi read the conclusion of the ceremony and advised the groom to stomp the glass.

Lifting Minnie in his arms, thrilled to his toes by what a featherweight she proved to be, Zelik carried her down the aisle past pews now filled with neighbors shouting, "Mazel tov!" With his thoughts turned toward their honeymoon, he carried his bride out of the synagogue to a manhole in the middle of North Main Street. But when he'd stepped into the tree and settled back into his skin, he found that he was empty-handed except for the branches he clung to for dear life.

The next day was agony all over again. Having never been drunk, Zelik thought this was what it must feel like to be hungover, so muddied in his brain were his memories of nocturnal derring-do. "Reckless shmeckless," he scoffed at himself Mr. Notowitz-style. Nervous and full of self-pity, he was valiant only in dreams.

Building a pyramid of apples in front of the market during the hottest part of the afternoon, Zelik pictured himself a slave in Egypt. Mr. Silver he tried to cast in the role of Pharaoh, which wasn't so easy given the grocer's recent high spirits. How could you account for such a change in the timid little man? Where he should have been bemoaning evil prospects for the future, here he was making plans.

"So, Zelik, I think maybe I'm purchasing to raise them in the yard some chickens. I would make a competition by Makowsky and Dubrovner that they could use a kick in the *toches*. Don't you agree?" Then he inquired as to what time the Rifkins might be walking to the park tonight.

Zelik had no opinions to speak of concerning Mr. Silver's business, but for all his discomfort, he wasn't unflattered that his opinion should have been sought. He even went so far as to make a pretense of weighing the matter thoughtfully.

Later, stepping into the hotbox of Mr. Notowitz's bedroom for his abortive Hebrew lesson, Zelik found the teacher poring feverishly over his texts. Stripped for once to his threadbare shirtsleeves, he was squeezing a boil on his neck with one hand, jotting notes and drawing diagrams in the broad margins with the other. When Zelik hemmed, the old man looked up and greeted him with unprecedented warmth.

"Ah, my prize pupil, make a guess what I do. Go ahead, make already a guess." Zelik opened his mouth to say that he hadn't a clue. "I, in my capacity that I call myself the Pseudo-

Abulafia, am hereby attempting the splitting of the Ineffable Name. So what you get when you do strictly by the formula from *The Kumquat Orchard* of Rabbi Velvl"—here he made a few more mad scribbles—"is you get for your trouble a fair likeness of the Cosmic Adam in his magic hat!"

"Come again," was all that Zelik could think to say.

But the old man's enthusiasm remained irrepressible. "So nu, what are you waiting?" he urged. "Give a look."

Zelik looked and saw a doodle resembling one of the multi-globed streetlamps along North Main, lit upon by a flock of crows. This he reported dutifully to Mr. Notowitz, who exhorted him to look again. "Don't tell to me you can't see him. Of course you can see him," the teacher assured his student, his optimism generating acid in Zelik's stomach. "Is possible, anything!"

Having deserted her sewing machine early that evening, Mrs. Rifkin was not to be found in the kitchen either. Zelik located her in her bedroom, primping in front of a mirror. She was mildly distressed at having nearly forgotten her Cousin (three times removed) Zygmund's Yahrzeit, who had died of something someplace far away.

"But what's the fuss, eh, *toteleh*? After all, the old *fortz* was cold before I got born. Now tell the truth, which do you prefer?" Holding up two kinds of earrings. "These ones or these with the thingamajigs that look like . . ." She laughed throatily, then blushed over what she thought they looked like.

Zelik was further bewildered at the attention paid him by his neighbors in Market Square. Before tonight, the most he could have expected from the citizens of North Main Street was their indifference, but now they hailed him with an amiable familiarity. They pinched his knobby shoulder and patted his back, gave him good-humored cuffs on the ear. Some paused to pass a little time in his company, asking his views on the affairs of the day: from the bull market to the films of Vilma Banky, the prospects for Prohibition repeal, the Monkey Trial, the duration of the heat wave, the fashionable positive thinking method of Dr. Emil Coué. When Zelik protested that he wasn't really up on current events, they pooh-poohed his modesty. And Minnie Alabaster blew him a kiss.

Her parents had stopped by the Rifkin bivouac to get Zelik's thoughts on a touring company currently playing the Orpheum Theater. This was when their daughter, posed beside them with one arm akimbo, touched her fingers to her full, pursed lips and blew in Zelik's direction. Stupefied, he slapped his cheek as if he'd actually felt the smack of her kiss, though it may have been only a coincidental mosquito bite.

What was happening, Zelik wondered, that everyone should be giving him such a red carpet treatment, after years of either ignoring him or making fun? Why this sudden about-face? They were a fickle bunch, his neighbors—that was all he could figure, and Minnie he deemed the most fickle of the lot. Another thing Zelik couldn't understand was how he could feel so crippled with exhaustion and still not be ready to sleep. He blamed the capriciousness of North Main Street for playing on his nerves. This was not to say he would have wanted them to fall back on their former disposition; it was just that this being regarded as a person, for whatever reasons, was new to him. It would take a little getting used to. In the meantime, the wisest course might be to stick to the shadows, keeping a safe distance from unpredictable neighbors, going where—once the park was quiet and he could rouse his aching bones—Zelik felt himself to be in control.

### MENSCH

While the summer never relented, the population of the Pinch seemed less oppressed by it than before. Something of the festive mood they displayed in the park at night was now extended to their daylight behavior. Rather than languish in helpless misery, they invented ways to beat the heat. They became less rigorous in observing their shop hours, taking siestas and making frequent trips to the public baths. Mrs. Bluestein designed a tunic made from twin enema bags filled with ice, which she threatened to have patented when it was copied by the Tailor Schloss. Another trend was set by Mr. Shapiro, who strung a hammock between his show racks, then hired neighborhood children to fan him with broad-brimmed fedoras. Everyone wore looser, skimpier garments, even pajamas and dressing gowns by day, lending North Main Street the aspect of a Baghdad seraglio. And one and all went out of their way to pay their respects to Zelik Rifkin.

With never a mention of any event that might have led to their change of heart, the shopkeepers sought him out. They asked his advice about embarrassingly personal matters, about the finer points of religious law as if he'd been a rabbi; they showed him a deference they might have accorded a local hero. Nor did they flinch at the improvised answers that Zelik had begun to find the temerity to hand them. Their wives dropped by to worry over him, agreeing with clucking tongues that the boy was too thin, plying him with pastries and noodle puddings that he should keep up his strength—though they never said what for. Sometimes they teased him that what he needed was a nice girl.

Grown accustomed to their attentions, Zelik had stopped wasting time in wondering whether he deserved them. What went on during business hours was of little concern to him, his days being only anxious preludes to his nocturnal escapades. After all, in the small hours, between foiling various nightmares, outmaneuvering Jakie Epstein along the way, he was with Minnie. A doting spouse, she'd set up housekeeping on a tiny painted ark drawn by swans in the Gayoso Bayou, and had begun to hint mysteriously that they might one day need an extra room. Reluctantly leaving her ardent embraces, Zelik set off on his self-appointed rounds of interfering in dreams. When there were no horrors to vanquish, he contented himself with making matches, such as the one between the bookish spinster, Miss Weintraub, and the handsome young novelist, F. Scott Fitzgerald, his first marriage having been annulled after his wife discovered his Jewish descent. All were in attendance at the reception atop the fleabag Cochran Hotel, where a lavish roof garden had miraculously appeared. There was a cake the size of a Carnival float, Kid Ory's Creole Band playing Old World klezmer standards, and Zelik himself in the role of wedding jester, using risqué material gleaned from his pretty bride in another life.

So, if the neighbors wanted to treat him like a celebrity, it was their affair. Zelik saw no reason why he ought to discourage them. Moreover, since his body had adjusted to its nightly dislocations and he was no longer bent double with pain, he was better prepared to receive their solicitous gestures.

Around the market these days, Mr. Silver, his perspiration glistening hair oil, hummed *freilachs* as he weighed the produce, striking cash register keys to end a refrain. He spoke now in a jovial singsong to his customers, attempting jokes which he generally mangled, tossing the bonus of an extra stringbean into their sacks. With his popular employee he liked to intimate how he had in mind a certain someone for a partnership, just as soon as that someone finished school.

"Incidentally," he would always inquire after his exchanges with Zelik, brushing off the freshly starched apron that Mrs. Rifkin had monogrammed, "what time do you and your mama walk tonight in Market Square?"

A little earlier every evening, Mr. Silver and Mrs. Rifkin—he in his spats with a hamper of laxative fruit, she all done up in her veiled cloche and high-vamped shoes—strolled to the park, shmoozing animatedly on the way. Zelik would trail behind them as discreetly as possible, given the attention he drew wherever he went. Sometimes Mr. Notowitz also joined their party, his informally open collar allowing the free sway of his wattled throat. Taking his student's arm, he might assure him he had the makings of an authentic *tzaddik,* and once paid Zelik the highest compliment: "I am seeing in you the young Aharon Notowitz." If the student reminded his teacher that he'd never before shown any special aptitude for learning, the old man insisted that such modesty was itself a sign of wisdom.

Then Zelik would have to gloat a bit despite himself, grinning complacently at the back of his mother's head. For the newly bobbed curls that peeked from under her hat, her coquettishness bespeaking a second girlhood, he felt in part responsible, though he couldn't say exactly how.

In another development, Jakie Epstein was sending around delegations inviting Zelik to attend various functions of the Gang. While making change or uncrating bananas (careless lately of tarantulas lurking among them), Zelik might feel a tug at his sleeve, then look up to find Augie Blot in his aviator goggles.

"Jakie wants to know if you'd like to be a umpire," he might say, spitting tobacco juice through a gap in his teeth; or, "Jakie wants to know if you'd like to watch us beat the kreplach out of the Mackerel Gang."

At first, Zelik tested the water gingerly, thinking he smelled something fishy. Since when had they ever requested his company except to make him the butt of a joke? But now, putting his suspicions to rest, they seemed genuinely pleased to see him, asking his advice about everything from placing policy bets to the speculated girth of Mrs. Kipper's bosom. Encouraged, Zelik began hanging around with the boys more often. He was tickled to have been accepted without having to spend the night on Beale Street or set fire to a schoolmistress or desecrate the Torah scrolls. But what was most appealing about his chumminess with the Pinch Gang was the opportunities it afforded Zelik to be close to Minnie.

Meanwhile, she was making unashamedly aggressive overtures toward him. She'd begun by targeting him as the special audience for her dubious humor ("So, Zelik, Doc Seligman walks into the deli and asks Mrs. Rosen if she's got hemorrhoids. 'Sorry, darling,' she says, 'only what's on the menu' "), then graduated to a more personal approach. "They say you been hiding your light under a bushel basket at Silver's," she might tease him, pouting provocatively. "Mind if I take a peek under your bushel?" Eventually even less circumspect, she would steal up behind him to whisper pet endearments: "*Zissskeit*, Sweet Patootie, my naughty Uncle Zelik, when are you coming to baby-sit your ickle Minnie?"

Always in his presence she managed to be fiddling with a stocking or dropping a scented handkerchief. Inhaling a lipstick-stained cigarette, she blew smoke rings that settled like halos over Zelik's head. And if the other boys, Jakie included, ever thought it unfair that the nebbish should command so much of Minnie's attention, they never let on.

Amazingly, Zelik wasn't frightened of her anymore. After a while he could weather her flirtations without his heart beginning to hum like a beehive whose vibrations he could feel in his pants. Cozy under his mantle of local maven, he forgot all those weeks of desperate yearning, and received her advances with a courtliness due the tender bride he knew her to be in her dreams.

He even found the nerve to return her flattery, if not quite in kind. "Minnie, you're a doll," he'd attempted on a note of confidence that fizzled when the words wouldn't come. "You're a . . . doll." But when the object of his tribute, instead of mocking him, winked as though the sally had struck home, Zelik was heartened. He could do no wrong. Moved to bolder experimentation, he cribbed lines from "The Song of Songs," domesticating them to the immediate surroundings.

"Thine eyes are as sunbeams in wine bottles," he extolled, reading what he'd scribbled on a shirt cuff with halting formality, "thy hair like when you lift the lid on a stove, thy teeth like freshly scrubbed stones in the potter's field. Thy neck is the obelisk in Confederate Park, thine *tsitskehs* a pair of puppies. The smell of thy garments is the smell of Ridblatt's Bakery. Behold, my *neshomeleh*, leaping on the cobbles, skipping on the shells of snapping turtles . . ."

Minnie rewarded him by squirming kittenishly, the words seeming to have touched her in intimate places. "Stop!" she pleaded, pulling her beret over her ears, after which she purred, "Sweetie, I'm yours!" Guilty of having kindled blushes in so many others, Minnie turned crimson herself, then grew sober: it was a grave responsibility to be thus adored. She dropped her forward manner and her trademark salty language, swapping them for an uncharacteristic hauteur. Having absorbed by association some of the fawning respect universally heaped on her "fella" (as Zelik was lately acknowledged to be), Minnie Alabaster began to put on airs.

It seemed to Zelik that he now had just about everything one could want in this world, and assumed it had all come about by the grace of his activities in another. But since his neighbors had never once referred to having seen him in their dreams, you might have argued otherwise. You could believe they'd simply come around to appreciating virtues in the kid that he himself hadn't recognized before.

At first, their homage had served only to violate his privacy; it distracted him from the driven anticipation of his nightly ascent up the oak. Nothing on earth was as beguiling or even, paradoxically, as real as what waited for him in the top of the tree. Then, the quality of life in the Pinch had changed: the neighbors ceased to utter discouraging words except about the weather. And, wonder of wonders, Minnie had given him her affection. Suddenly, the daylight North Main Street was making a bid to compete with its nocturnal counterpart. In fact, they were neck and neck, and Zelik, drawn irresistibly to each, was never so content as to spend his days in one and his nights in the other.

Honored in the greengrocery, he still went through his stockboy's motions, though he was often interrupted by neighbors dropping by to bend his ear. Mr. Silver, if he worried about anything, worried that his assistant might become fatigued. With a paternal interest in Zelik's welfare, not to say a newfound sympathy for matters of the heart, he would advise his employee to take off early and go visit his girl.

A creature of habit, Zelik never failed to look in on Mr. Notowitz, whom he frequently found in the throes of mystical transport, naked but for his holey underwear. "Here by the gate of paradise is Notowitz!" the old man might proclaim, the sparse hair horizontal at his temples. "Behold that it is as an elevator up the trunk of the Tree of Life—I'm talking my room. You are maybe wanting to ride?" Zelik, who never rode when he could climb, would tell the teacher, "I'll take a rain check," then excuse himself and hurry off to preside over the doings of the Pinch Gang.

With Minnie on his arm he was practically holding court, a solemn and discerning presence at their assorted pranks and brawls. They even made sure he had a grandstand view of their more disreputable enterprises—the bootlegging, the petty thefts. For himself Zelik was happy to turn a blind eye to such proceedings, but sometimes, lest they offend her sensibilities, he thought it better to lead Minnie away. He took her for walks to show her off along streets where he had previously wandered in stealth all alone; and in the evenings, touching fingertips to each other's lips, the sweethearts exchanged a fond goodnight. The moment seemed all the more delicate against the backdrop of the noisy park, its racket increased by the conspicuous billing and cooing of Mrs. Rifkin and the grocer. Afterward, when everyone else was bedded down and sleeping, Zelik would climb the tree and meddle in their dreams.

It was heaven on earth, this bounty he now enjoyed, though it had somewhat displaced the sweet suspense of waiting each day for night to fall. Lately, while his body still longed in every fiber to make the climb, Zelik, his mind becalmed, wondered what was the hurry. Owing to his popularity, the neighbors had relocated their encampments until the Rifkins replaced the oak as centerpiece of the gathered community. This made it chancier to go creeping among them. Moreover, should anyone catch him climbing, what with their great concern for his welfare, they would insist he come down at once before hurting himself. And sometimes it occurred to Zelik that, for their sakes, maybe he ought to be a bit more careful.

Also, when you thought of it, his meteoric rise to respectability rivaled anything he'd encountered in dreams. Dreams could scarcely improve on the bliss that was Zelik's daily fare. In coming to share his neighbors' estimation of himself, he felt almost as if North Main Street, in both its terrestrial and celestial manifestations, belonged to him; as if all that went on in that neighborhood above the sleeping park were contained in a dream of Zelik's own. Or was it an hallucination, since who wouldn't see things if they'd missed as much sleep as he?

Then came a night when the thought of his marathon wakefulness made him yawn. All around him his neighbors were already deep in slumber, and exposed as he was, Zelik figured it must be catching. Maybe a short nap would refresh him for the climb. Yawning luxuriously, he stretched out on the davenport that Shafetz's Discount had donated for his comfort. (His mother had been provided a chaise longue.) With his fingers locked behind his head, eyes closed to the shooting stars, he began to doze, falling into a dream about Minnie. In it he was dissatisfied with their hand-holding dalliance, and had begun despite her protests to fumble under her clothes. He was jolted awake to a throbbing sense of something unfinished, but presently succumbed to drowsiness again.

### A CHANGE IN THE WEATHER

In the days following the abandonment of his nightly climb, Zelik looked forward to sleeping as much as he'd previously looked forward to scaling the oak. He slept long and deep, and in the mornings had to be roused by his mother with persistent shaking. Throughout the rest of the day he took every occasion to catnap, catching his winks where he might, convinced that his record insomnia had finally caught up with him. Meanwhile, his neighbors continued to greet him affably enough, though they sometimes caught themselves in midsentence, pausing in irritation as if suddenly aware of having transgressed some personal code. Frequently stuporous, however, Zelik was the last to notice that their attitude toward him had grown chillier and more remote.

Even his closest acquaintances got into the act. There was the afternoon, for instance, when, sacked out for a snooze on a cooler at the rear of the market, Zelik was rudely awakened by the grocer. "Stop with the loafing already," snapped Mr. Silver, his cheeks sagging from the weight of the bags under his eyes. "Troubles I got enough of without I should have a goldbrick on the job."

Hitting a snag in his mystical investigations—the critical twelfth combination of the letters of the Tetragrammaton having failed to induce the visionary state—Mr. Notowitz, who'd reverted to his mossgrown suit, blamed his difficulties on his student's untimely entrance.

"Where you been, you never heard of knocking?" he demanded, rapping his forehead with a bony fist until he'd raised a lump. "Come in, Mr. Rifkin, that he walks in the way of the Torah repairing its breaches. Better he should walk in the way of his mama repairing britches." Violently blowing his nose in the crook of his sleeve.

Dowdy again in a washed-out housefrock, her face lackluster in the absence of shadow and rouge, Mrs. Rifkin asked her son if he'd mind correcting the tilt of her neglected calendar. And while he was at it, he should tear off the July page, since August was already half over, though where the time had gone she didn't know.

There was also discontent in the ranks of the Pinch Gang, who'd begun to express impatience with the way Zelik remained always the spectator. It started one late afternoon on the levee, when Ike, the semi-articulate twin, asked Zelik, "How come you don't never do nothing but sit and look?" Seated on a bollard with Minnie beside him, her elbow resting on his shoulder, Zelik rolled his eyes in a groggy smirk. He expected the others to do the same rather than dignify such a stupid question. But Jakie himself, drying off after a dip in the river, his stringy muscles atwitch in his soaking skivvies, seconded the Lieberman's query. This left it to the irreverent Augie Blot to set them straight.

" 'Cause he's a rare bird, ain't you heard? A yellow-bellied Zelik." He went on to call him names intended to dissolve any lingering illusion that the emperor was wearing clothes.

Zelik puffed himself up, speechless at Augie's show of insubordination. Truly, it was a harsher judgment than the others seemed prepared to accept, and with a pop of the jaw Jakie offered the accused a chance to allay their suspicions.

"Whyn't you dive off the crane if you ain't afraid?"

Swallowing hard, Zelik maintained his composure. "What for should I want to get all wet?"

When Augie suggested he already was, Minnie cut him short, forgetting herself in a curse that dismissed Jakie's mouthpiece as a pink-eyed, limp-*petseled* bed-wetter. Then, swelling the bodice of her sailor blouse, she was haughty again. "Go ahead, sweetie, give the monkeys a thrill." She patted her mouth in a yawn, bored at the prospect of yet another example of her boyfriend's fearlessness.

Aggravated, wanting a nap, Zelik turned to remind his companion that he didn't have to prove himself, when he saw in the set of her features that he must. Petulantly, he slid from the bollard and kicked off his shoes. He removed his cap and shirt, handing them to Minnie, who received them as if this were part of an established routine. Aware of how his pallor contrasted with the sun-tanned bodies of the Gang, he was also conscious of the fact that Jakie Epstein didn't have a corner on knotty biceps, Zelik's clandestine tree-climbing activities having whipped him into pretty fair shape.

He strolled up to the greasy travelling platform from which a tall crane leaned out over the river, and sprang onto the ladder. In seconds he was scrambling up the girders of the crane itself, using the large bolts encrusted with pigeon *drek* for toe-holds, climbing with an easy agility. Then it was bracing to demonstrate before an audience what had become for

Zelik an almost involuntary exercise; although, as he mounted higher, he discovered he was a little out of practice. He was slightly winded as he neared the top, not to say dizzy from the contraption's tilt and sway, and the sun, glinting off the tin roofs of houseboats and the river, stung his eyes whenever Zelik dared to look down. Here he awoke to the realization that, for all his dream heroics, he had yet to disprove the famous Rifkin chickenheartedness by day. It was a truth that stopped him cold, left him clinging to the girders for dear life, listening to insults hurled from the cobbles and feeling his nose begin to bleed.

After that, Minnie became increasingly difficult to live with, though she continued to stick by Zelik with a stubborness that challenged anyone to so much as look askance. But where her beau had turned back before her eyes into a milquetoast, Minnie had begun to act the floozy again. She'd revived her teasing manner that called into question the virility of the other boys, sometimes suckering them into flirtations which she abruptly thwarted. Once more she was telling stories that cast their families in compromising roles: "So Nathan Shapiro meets his papa coming out of a bordel on Beale Street, and his papa says, 'Don't be angry, sonny. Would you want I should wake your mama at such an hour for a dollar?' " And always she looked over her shoulder for Zelik's reaction.

Then the first time he'd presumed to suggest that this kind of behavior wasn't becoming, Minnie turned on him. She yanked him behind the Market Square bandstand and offered him another chance to prove his mettle. "What do you say, my big strong ape-mensch," she breathlessly invited, watering Zelik's eyes with her cheap perfume, "won't you give your angelfood girlie a little fun?"

"I don't know what's got into you, Minnie." Zelik tried to stand firm in his disapproval, though neither of them was fooled. Both understood that he was simply afraid to touch her, at least in her fleshly daylight incarnation.

"Okay, kiddo," sniffed Minnie, twisting her neck to admire the bare shoulder that her boat-necked blouse revealed, "If you can't show me a good time, there's others who can." Pausing to light a cigarette, she flicked the match at Zelik before traipsing off.

Brooding but undaunted, Zelik resolved to fix things the next time he saw her, if not here on earth then elsewhere. He determined to make good again in dreams what he'd botched in waking life. How had he let the situation get so out of hand in the first place? It was true of course that, during his drowsy absence, the street at the top of the oak had all but faded into unreality; but now this only increased Zelik's urgency to reconfirm what had to have been more than just the fruits of an overwrought imagination.

At dusk on the same day that Minnie had called his bluff, however, there was a distinctly literal chill in the air. There was a breeze that the neighbors were welcoming as the harbinger of an early autumn, their reward for having survived such a scorching summer.

"Thank God that tonight in our own beds we will sleep," sighed Mr. Silver, who had recently begun talking about Klan raids in the park again.

"What are you saying!" cried his young assistant, on hand to panic. "This summer ain't over by a longshot. You'll see, the temperature'll soar. Don't be taken in by a little breeze."

The grocer was perplexed that anyone should seem to want the heat to endure. "Meshuggah," he grumbled, turning away, washing his hands of an employee who, beyond feckless, was crazy to boot.

Zelik wandered up North Main Street listening to the shopkeepers trading expressions of relief over the change in the weather. Taking every opportunity to contradict them, he insisted they shouldn't relax: "Don't you know we're in for more of the same?" But the neighbors only shook their heads, no longer influenced by what the screwball Rifkin kid might believe.

That night Zelik went to the empty park all alone. Not only had the wind picked up, with a blustery edge that gave him gooseflesh, but a fierce storm was threatening. Huge, billowing thunderheads obscured the moon, their interiors lit like intermittent X rays. Then the sky cracked open and a gullywasher ensued. Running home in the torrential downpour, fording gutters flash-flooded to his knees, Zelik was drenched to the marrow. Even changed into his nightshirt and nestled under the covers, he couldn't stop trembling.

At first unable to sleep, he fell at length into an agitated insensibility, dreaming that the oak was struck by lightning at its crown, riven limbs tumbling to earth in sizzling flames. He woke up sopping all over again, the sheets clammy from his sweat. For an instant Zelik thought his prayers had been answered: the heat had returned with an intensity that made a furnace of the apartment. But how could this be, when the rain was still drumming away in the alley outside? It was a mystery that goaded Zelik into abandoning his bed for the cluttered living room. His mother and Mr. Notowitz, a sheet draped like a prayer shawl over his shoulders, were already at the windows, looking onto a stormy North Main Street aglow beneath a hyacinth-orange sky.

The word went from building to building that the great wooden barn of the Phoenix Athletic Club had been struck by lightning. "It went up just like matchsticks," was the word. Although the boxing arena stood a block away on Front Street, the heat from its conflagration was so furious that the windows of the Rifkin apartment were too hot to touch. Over the clanging engines from five alarms, you could hear the nickering screams of horses in a stable near the arena that had also caught fire. You could hear the sound of shattering glass as windows were bursting all over the Pinch.

JACOB'S LADDER

For a day or so it was hard to tell whether the overcast sky was due to dark clouds or the smoke from the smoldering arena. But soon the cooler air blew away the smoke, the sun reappeared, and the season turned.

By now Zelik's status in the community had degenerated from merely discredited to outcast. Nostalgic for his former condition of near-invisibility, he lurked in backstreets, avoiding as best he could the scornful glances of his neighbors, the taunts of Jakie's gang. From the way everyone behaved, you'd have thought he was personally responsible for whatever disappointment they'd experienced in life.

To make matters worse, Zelik's friend and employer, reeling from a recent attack of gentile phobia, informed his so-called assistant that he would have to lay him off. "It ain't so hotsy-totsy, the produce business," explained Mr. Silver.

Zelik put up a token resistance. "So what happened to 'With a certain cute boychik, I am making a partnership?'"

"That was couple weeks ago already," said the grocer, pausing a moment to plaintively recall the past. "To tell the truth, what it is that ain't good for business is you."

Neither was it good for business, thought Zelik, that Mr. Silver shook in his bluchers every time some yokel walked in from the wagon yard. And what about his recent quarrel with Mrs. Rifkin? (It had begun trivially enough with the seamstress accusing her suitor of having falsely advertised inferior merchandise, but had ended in the mutual dissolution of their romance.) Let Silver deny that had anything to do with the sudden dismissal of his faithful employee. But Zelik wasn't really inclined to argue. The job had entailed more public exposure than he had the heart to suffer, and, besides, who needed the grocer's penny-ante charity?

Meanwhile Mr. Notowitz's experiments in practical kabbalah had entirely broken down, and the old teacher had withdrawn into a sullen and demon-ridden silence. If he emerged for meals, he ate little; he complained that feasting all summer on the fruit of the Tree of Life had given him terminal gas. As for Mrs. Rifkin, with the courtship of Leon Silver blotted from

her memory, she'd resumed her fanatical devotion to the calendar of events in other people's lives.

As the following months ushered in the bitter winter of
Zelik's discontent, no one else in the Pinch appeared to be
doing much better. Everyone griped that business had fallen
off. They blamed their lack of prosperity—which was a new
line, as if they'd just woken up to the fact that they were
poor—on the treachery of their Irish and Italian competitors;
though the butcher Makowsky was heard to say of the butcher
Dubrovner, who promptly returned the compliment, that he
was not above certain underhanded practices of his own. Most
agreed with Mr. Silver that the mayor of Memphis, a self-styled
potentate nicknamed the Red Snapper, was perfectly capable
of reinstituting the blood libel. A pogrom might be imminent.

But of all the available scapegoats on which the neighborhood pinned their woes, Zelik Rifkin remained a sentimental
favorite, the Pinch's own resident Jonah. The latest complaint
to become popular along North Main Street was chronic insomnia, which had infected enough to be declared an epidemic. Despite unusually cold weather otherwise suited for a
deep winter's hibernation, the neighbors grew ever more irri-
table from loss of sleep. For this they were also disposed to
blame the Rifkin kid, though direct expressions of annoyance
had to be reserved for the rare occasions when he was sighted.
Thus, having once been revered for no apparent reason, Zelik
was now just as unreasonably despised.

The worst was, of course, that Minnie wanted nothing to
do with him. In the face of her active disdain, however, Zelik's
pining for the ginger-haired *shainkeit* had, if anything, intensi-
fied. But this was not the wistfully chivalrous brand of longing
that had kept him satisfied in the days when he was secure in
her adoration. Now Zelik wanted to encircle her slender waist
and squeeze for all he was worth. He wanted to nibble her
succulent earlobe, bury his nose in the warmth of her boobies,
bite the delectable flesh above her rolled stocking while mur-

muring forbidden words. He cursed and berated himself for the opportunities he'd let slip by, for neglecting to act on the nerve that he'd deceived himself into thinking he had.

Leaning out of doorways in his earflaps and ulster, parting racks of pants gone stiff from the chilly air, Zelik spied on Minnie. He watched her gossiping as she left Levy's Candy Store with Rose Padauer and Sadie Blen, heard her twitting the boys with her racy remarks, the choicest of which she'd begun to save for Jakie Epstein. Holding his breath so its steam wouldn't give him away, he saw Minnie urge Jakie to drop back from the others, tugging him into an alley where they could bundle and pet. But try as he might, Zelik was never able to picture himself in the place of the daredevil captain of the Gang.

The unending cold snap did nothing to take the edge off his terrible wanting, and eventually a day arrived when desire got the better of fear. Having waited for the lovebirds to part company in a gravel drive behind the cigar factory, Zelik pitched forward through a sprinkling of snowflakes to block Minnie's path.

"M-n-n-n." His chattering teeth prevented him from getting beyond a blue-lipped approximation of her name.

Hugging herself in her mackinaw against the raw January wind, Minnie wondered aloud, "What did I ever see in you? *Gevalt!*" She slapped her brow with a mittened palm. "I must of had a hole in my head."

In the instant before she started away, Zelik saw in her emerald eyes that she scarcely even considered him worth pitying. Frantically hoping that a second look might erase the first, he lunged for her arm and spun her around.

"Nobody!" she hissed. "You got wet *lokshen* where your backbone ought to be."

He was sobbing when he embraced her, the sobs mounting to a caterwaul as they tussled, as he tried to thrust his fingers between the buttons of her coat. It was a clumsy assault, too blind and confused to be effective, and Minnie handily repulsed him with a knee to his groin. He slumped against a bill-plastered wall and slid to the gravel, Minnie already showing him her heels, though she turned back briefly to deliver a kick for good measure to his shin. While the hot tears cooled to an icy glaze on his cheeks, Zelik surrendered to the contemplation of his basest act of cowardice so far.

Warmer weather brought little relief, though with a heady bouquet of growing things in the air, the open hostility of his neighbors toward Zelik seemed to have subsided. His disgrace, lacking any sound basis in circumstance, was apparently forgotten along with the dreadful winter, and the street resumed its original indifference to the Rifkin kid. Not that it mattered. By now Zelik had more than enough disgust for himself to compensate for what his neighbors no longer took the trouble to feel.

He had for some time discontinued his spying operations, leaving home only to attend the Market Avenue School, in whose dusty corridors and classrooms he'd perfected his nonentity. Otherwise, except on those evenings when he accompanied her to the synagogue for prayers and *Yizkor* services, Zelik remained his mother's shut-in companion. He let his days be defined, like hers, by the calendar of banner events—a new calendar published by a company that made wrought iron anvils. Avoiding their cranky boarder, Zelik occupied himself with daydreams in which nobody ever turned out a hero, though sometimes, if only to break the monotony, he might be moved to inquire about the relatives they mourned. Maybe one of them had had an interesting life. But in the end he dropped the questions, having confirmed that his toilworn mother hardly knew any more about them than he.

School let out and spring turned imperceptibly to summer, a mild summer like an apology for the previous year's inferno. But the balmy days were too good to last, and somewhere around mid-July the heat was once again cranked up full force. The shopkeepers lolled in their sweaty undershirts, their faces hidden beneath wet rags. On their noggins they wore newspapers folded into admiral's hats, smeared head-lines declaring no end in sight for the dog days. The *k'nackers* claimed they were dredging boiled mussels from the river, that Kaplan the realtor had cornered the market in shade, while the pious tended to view the heat wave as a *finsternish,* another plague visited for their sins on North Main Street by an angry God. Eentsy Lazarov had been spotted in the arms of her *shegetz* in the balcony of the Orpheum Theater, Morris Hano-ver seen departing a hog-nosed cafe on Beale Street eating tref. Though if it occurred to anyone to blame the unbearable weather on Zelik Rifkin, they were never heard to say.

Like every other apartment in the Pinch, the one above Silver's Fruit & Veg was practically beyond habitation. Its oc-cupants were unable to draw a breath without feeling as if someone else had drawn it before them; there seemed not enough of that torpid air to go around. This, Zelik told him-self, was what he deserved, though the heaviness of the after-noon in question left him wondering if there might be a limit even for him. Raising himself from his prostration atop a pile of clothes in need of mending, he panted hopefully, "Did anybody die today?"

With barely the strength to pump the treadle on her hob-bling machine, Mrs. Rifkin glanced at the calendar. "Your Great Uncle Gershon," she sighed.

Of Uncle Gershon Zelik knew only that he'd perished long ago in some unpronounceable village in Europe, and that his memorial meant he and his mother, please God, would leave the apartment tonight. It never entered his head anymore that he might go out alone.

Because it was *Shabbos,* the whole of North Main Street was in the synagogue, flapping their *siddurs* like an aviary to try and stir a breeze. There were several instances of fainting, not to be confused with swoons in the gallery during the cantor's megaphone vocals. Dehydrated babies wailed and *daveners* gib-bered in no identifiable tongue. Finally Rabbi Fein, so *farshvitst* you'd have thought his bowler was an upturned bucket, hauled himself onto the bima to deliver his benedictory sermon. Wrapped in his wringing tallis like a bath towel, he reeled as he recited what purported to be a midrash on the subject of Jacob's Ladder.

" . . . You had at the bottom of the ladder the angels, that they looked like old men in their caftans, their wings scrawny as a chicken's. But the closer they are getting, these angels, to the top of the ladder, the more antsy-pantsy and fuller of pep they become. Then it's off with the clothes, they're throwing them willy-nilly, and hallelujah! youthful figures they got now, with lovely wings that make a nice cool breeze . . ."

The rabbi cleared his throat and recovered his composure. "The lesson from this text we are learning," he began with authority; then his eyes started to shift and he muttered hastily that the congregation were free to draw their own conclusions. He raised his voice to announce that the ladies of the synagogue auxiliary would be on hand with provisions for those who elected to stay the night in Market Square.

### THE CEILING OF FATE

Too depleted from the ordeal of the service to protest, Mrs. Rifkin allowed her son to lead her across the street into the park. There they joined the others milling about like survivors of a shipwreck, receiving from the ladies blankets for making pallets and collapsible cups of iced tea. On the far edge of the circle of neighbors, Zelik spread the blanket and saw that his wilting mother was settled comfortably for the night. Sitting beside her, he patted his chest through his shirt in an effort to quiet the frightened fluttering within.

Everyone was there: Mr. Silver beneath the lilac with his galluses hanging, swilling stomach bitters to chase down his prunes; Mr. Notowitz disguised as refuse on his bench. Some members of the Pinch Gang could be seen shadow-boxing under the tree, a knot of girls (Zelik wondered if Minnie were among them) conspiring nearby. Now and then neighbors passed seeking extra hands for card games, looking to stake claims on unoccupied pieces of ground, but not one gave the Rifkin kid so much as a "Howdoyado." They ignored Zelik so completely he might have doubted his very existence, which, under the circumstances, he found somehow reassuring.

In the moonless sky, however, there were occasional flashes of lightning, promising rain, threatening to reduce the oak to a burning bush. Zelik could feel this particular worry beginning to spawn others until he was permeated with a general dread. Over and over, as the neighbors extinguished their lanterns and allowed their Victrolas to wind down, he had to remind himself that this was only heat lightning, which was nothing but the echo of a storm too far away to matter.

To his mother he whispered, in order not to wake her, "Goodnight, Mama, I'm off to climb a tree to the Land of Nod," then started at her mumbled words of caution. He got to his feet and made his way among his neighbors, casting rueful glances at their recumbent forms, as if they'd fallen in battle instead of merely fallen asleep.

He stepped onto a root and jumped, clambering painfully aloft. Due to a long inertia, his muscles were unused to climbing, never mind the state of his nerves, and Zelik groaned his torment at every stage of the ascent. Too scared to look down, he nevertheless managed to lose his footing from time to time, and had to hug the tree until his breath returned. Somewhere during the climb his groans turned to whimpers, though after a certain height Zelik's suffering began to sound in his own ears as if it belonged to someone else.

When he'd surfaced from under the fog, he filled his lungs with courage, his eyes with crazy dreams. Slipping neatly out of his body, Zelik stood astride the manhole to watch the shenanigans of North Main. The Widow Teitlebaum was on her balcony, serenaded by a cowboy bearing a marked resemblance to Cantor Abrams in Stetson and chaps. Sacharin the herring-monger tossed handbills from on board a flying fish, and Lazar the red-whiskered bootlegger, unscrewing a fire plug, deluged the gutters with an amber flood of beer. But anxious as he was to commence his rounds, Zelik restrained himself; there was a piece of business he had first to attend to.

Dropping back into the tree, he hung by his knees and surveyed the park below. From this topsy-turvy vantage Zelik felt almost as if he were at the bottom of the oak again, looking up into a dark canopy hung with dreamers. He judged that all was as it should be with them, just as it was with his own outmoded self, fearfully clutching the branches under the ceiling of fog. Reaching down, Zelik took hold of those tenacious fingers and endeavored to pry them loose. Then his old golf-capped, knee-pantsed, skin-and-bones double struggled to retain its balance. To make sure that it didn't, Zelik gave it a little shove. As he swung back up onto the airborne pavement, he heard the thrashing beneath him, the desolate shriek, which he muffled by sliding the iron manhole cover into place. Nothing remained after this but to stroll off into the thick of things. **Q**

## Ram Farm

### HOOKS IN THE WALL

They took me to see some bulls in a barn. A man there held open a gate. A bull moved around a little in its kell. The bulls had black faces and white creases under the eyes. They picked up a stick and poked a bull in the face. The bull moved around a little and made a sound. It curled back its black eyeball. They waved for me. They pointed to a scar on the bull. They took me to another room in the barn. This one had hanging straps, harnesses. There were metal drums and tubs, smocks hanging on a peg. There was the head of a bull in the wall with an apple in its mouth. There was a gun on a slab. They picked up the gun and they pointed the muzzle at their necks, shrugged up their cheeks and chins, shut their eyes. They fell on their backs on the floor. They made cracking sounds, breathing out of their mouths. There were some skins on bricks by a gate. They were piled and lumpy in the shape of a bull. They opened their eyes and smiled. They pointed to tall boys outside. Then they took me to see more bulls.

### THE MORNING

Lips, kidneys, liver, heart, skin, neck. Other parts of the body are eaten, too—hooves, hair, brain, jowls, snout, tongue, stomach, tail. Hog blood is used to make food. Hog bones are ground or shaved. People need glue and oil. Some hog tails are wet with little shoots that cut your hand. Some hogs frown when they are in pain. My father once made his face that way to show me. Yorkshires, Berkshires, Hampshires, Lambshires, Spotted Swine—these are kinds of hogs. These are names of hogs on the farm: Holy Roland, Roly Joe. It is good luck to use the name of a man who lived a long life. The way a hog grunts can make it seem the hog is saying your name. Lump Jaw, Hark Jar, Cholera, Bang's, and Mange. Muscle, tendon, and bone make up the feed. Almost everything is eaten. You can eat slices of the liver fried, plus hot blackberry sauce and pear cream on the side. The brain can be boiled with vinegar and celery root. Add gingersnap sauce or rub with a lemon. Hold it under cold water, scrubbing it the way my father did—brushing in small circles with the thumb. Make a flour paste and use bell peppers. I admired their size. I admired their strength. The bodies of hogs! I thought that the pigs slept inside the hogs at night. You can touch the spot in the air right here where one once was.

### THE WOMEN IN THE WINDOW

The hogs come up this way, side by side, rubbly, bucking up their faces. They are happy! The hogs in the morning—past pigs, snouts into a sow, and hogs eating at the creep socket, and hogs through the creep slat. The hogs running—a leg up this way, a kind of grin, a leg up this way, a tusk, a flak of dirt. The hogs duck, bump, coming for us, their hair in sharp ends, their hips just hair and a crease. The hogs! The hogs come up to us this way, almost falling over, seeming almost to tiptoe, ready to line up tonight outside our house, lobbing rocks at the shingles, one by one, over their shoulders, fancily, without looking at what they want to hit.

### RAM

The bark rake, the pig rack, the pigeon gill—I remember the barn. The barn was in the First Corner, and they called the First Corner the Fist Corner. We watched a shot bull roll in the palm! A horse also died right here, right in the middle of eating off a boy's foot. Green Lat had made the horse's face bleed and its belly black. A boy with no arms once bent over and trembled out his tongue to touch his toe, for one dollar. Somebody chased him away from the barn. The bark rake on the barn made one of the fingers a flap of wood—and were you afraid of all you could fall under all day the way I was? The fire, the broom, the father—claws and the tub through the ceiling the next time! The portrait on the wall of the father carrying the son, the son seeming to fall even in the portrait—in the house in the Second Corner. They called the Second Corner the Sick Corner, and the Bone or Point or Elbow. The mother was dead. They lifted me up to see. Our house was in the Third Corner, and they called the Third Corner Schwartz. The house, the door, the rail—I remember the rusted window silver, the crusted shit by the sitz cow! They also called our corner the Shoulder—and the grass slope was the high, meat part of an arm. The cracks in the dirt were the veins. They called all of Ram Farm God's Arm. I was afraid.

### ROPE TAIL

My father brought up a dog before breakfast and had the dog call up at the boys who were standing on the roof, cracking ice. It was so cold there in the morning! One of the men would squeeze on my hat and tug my ears and give me a cinnamon hook after lunch. My father once sat on a bike backward. I knew what the girl kneeled for. Look at the snow! The men would dig us out and sometimes a horse would come with us. My father sometimes stood on a rung of a gate and held his hands together to sing down at the pigs. One of the boys pinned a pig's legs back. I wore a sailor's blouse! One of the men used a bucket under the bull, cutting, pulling from the bull. One of the boys showed the trick in his hand—the brad, the penny, the thumb covered up. There were so many men there! The same man would always lift me by my armpits at night and carry me along the rail of the steps. A boy would help me into the house. My father would shut the door. **Q**

### *Father*

"Made you some furniture," he says.

"Yeah?" I ask.

"Yeah." He stands on one foot, looking down. "Can I come in?" he asks.

On the stairs he is shorter than I am.

"I don't need any furniture," I say.

"I know," he says. "Can I come in? I could fix your phone for you."

"I don't think so," I say.

"Yeah," he says, looking at his watch. "Made a couple chairs and a table." He looks over at my car in the driveway. "Also, a dresser and a desk. You need a desk maybe?" He turns toward me hopefully.

I shake my head.

"I figured," he sighs. "Figured you wouldn't." He steps down one step. "Well." Another step. "You just call me if you need anything, okay?"

I nod.

He goes down the last step and walks to his car. He looks at me again, then gets in and drives away. I watch him go. **Q**

The superman trials

## Neither Moth Nor Rust

You see it was impossible.
Death was worse than all
the books my mother returned
on time. So the fines added up

till the day of her funeral.
Now the unexpected guests
arrive, poor as they are,
taking her china and crystal.

## The Bait

Adam fishing in a lake,
his genitals floating
in the reeds—cut off
at the waist, a double-
minded lure suspended
between two worlds, Eve
rising up from under.

## *Consolation*

Don't want to go out. The toilet
growing dark with mold. Wax fruit
on a plate. Have learned to keep
things simple. Nothing I cannot fix.
My hair. A button. Whatever helps

me sleep. A slow drip from the tap.
Something constant. Clear. Not
wanting to strike a match. Or make
decisions. The weight of my head
in my hands, old linen on the table.

## The Kore

What was sacred was in my journey
the whole way back, leaving her
in pieces the way I had found her.

## White Train

On Railroad Avenue you could see this
lady wearing a white bra and half-slip
standing at a window without the shade drawn.
This was the way sometimes
an ordinary glance turned into a vision
that made you feel destined for something.

At six o'clock in the morning
men are waiting in front of the tavern,
stamping their feet as if to drive the cold
back into the ground. At night the bedrooms
are awash in the light of televisions.
But this was before television.

The war was heard on a radio
shaped like a church. I dreamed
of my father falling out of the sky.
Winter arrived like a white train.
Looking out the windows, the passengers
seemed to have certain answers.

I remember the gleam of light on linoleum
floors where I played with a tin wind-up toy.
You end up praising what is lost
merely in hopes of being reconciled.
I pretended it was my father stepping off the train,
and it was.

## His Insomnia

He shuffled cards all night long
or rearranged the furniture,
although the next morning it was
in the same place as before.

His bed had the aura of a bridge
from which someone moments ago
had jumped. In my imagination
his pillow was black.

A car swerving almost out of control
threw sudden lights and shadows
on the walls, the ceiling.
My dreams felt scratched on me.

I pictured his insomnia
as a tiny blue flame
wavering
inside his head.

Sometimes the furniture was covered
with sheets as in a vacant house,
and the draperies concealed a body
in the shape of their folds.

He wore the remnants
of a uniform. You could not tell
what color it had been, except
where the insignia were removed.

## Burning Windows

After the sneak attack, my uncle
was one of the many customers
who jammed the Acme Liquor Store,
anticipating a shortage.

He read the lumps on my head
as a legend of ingratitude.
He paid the $44 a month for
our apartment on Railroad Avenue.
But I had seen them screwing.

At night, on the other side
of the blackout curtain, I imagined
houses in flame,
their windows burning.

I helped my mother bake cookies
she called "hearts of stone."
I went with my uncle when he went
to church to keep what he called
his "tendencies" in check.

He had a little spyglass,
and when you looked into it
you saw a naked woman.
I am ashamed to say I prized it
more than I did my father's medals.

*Card Shark*

I can see why ancient writers made
their oracles blind. There was something
about the notion of their seeing
that remained unseen—you cannot
imagine that any man can really
foretell the future unless he at least
close his eyes. Being blind
must be better.

            The best poker player
I ever saw was blind. I saw
you had four clubs, he said. He laughed
about that.

            He had alligator shoes,
and I asked him what pleasure he got
out of that. A certain feeling
about how they shine.

            Feeling is right,
he said. I can feel the shine.
The way I imagine the future,
feeling my way along the dark and imagine
the way someone like you, with clearest
eyes, will see it, or not see it.
I've never seen the moon. I don't
know what these poets are talking about
when they shimmer up the moon like a big
ball of ice. I can see four clubs
exposed on the table. They're cards.
I've felt clubs like clovers in the grass.
Moons I have no feelings for.

            I can stand
miscalculation; I can understand

misunderstanding—someone looking up
at that rock and thinking it was
magical the way it ran across the sky
and even stood out at noonday like a coin.
These things people have told me,
and I know a coin. But the sky—what
is sky? Blue? I'm also color-blind.
I don't know blue or white for clouds.
Colors? Red? A trumpet. Hardly.
When I go to sleep, I dream
in words, no pictures, smells, yes,
but they're not attached to anything.
Who dreams in smells anyway? Just words,
sounds, people talking, nothing like pictures
as far as I know anything about pictures.
Stars you say spangle the skies like snowflakes
I feel as they strike my eyes and light
on me as chill as salt. Sky? What's up?
You go up, up. Of course, you only feel
you go up because you see it. To me it is
like riding on a train. I hardly know up,
that heavy lifting of the plane, and the roar
gives me some idea of the expanse of it,
up like the heave of a giant shovel. I'm blind,
I see the future, it glows around me as reaction.
It shines like my alligator shoes
or perhaps like the sun (I have no notion
of that except the warmth on my skin).
I go through a fever like that, like the cat
from pot to pot never stepping on the floor.
I see what you feel, black as it is.

I move in my mind. I lift my brainish foot
and never touch what I never want to use.
You see? You see.

　　　　　　　He smiled. I know you
have four clubs—only four, and I have
two aces. I only know the cards. I see them.

## A Poem for My Fingers

I turn from my perch in the sepia morning,
And dive into her. Entering at the sternum.
Plunging into the river of her sleep.
The fall rips my arms from their sockets.
I swim on, a seal freed from the tyranny
Of hands, no holding or pencils or shoelaces,
Not even thought, as if thumbs were
Where the brain resides.
Coursing along until the dawn brings
Shore.

## My Woman

I have a twin whose navel shows
The breaking of the stem, the wrenched
Junction whose depression matches my
Elevation exactly, who has a secret
I know, have entered, have occupied,
Have rested in that
Limpid place.

## *Metaphor*

I've always
wanted to write
a poem with
boats and sails,
maybe using them
as a metaphor,
but I don't know shit
about any of that.

## To Maurice Eidelsberg

I know
what you mean
I know
where
it comes from
but
I can't get
any either.

**MICHAEL KIMBALL**

## Places I Have Been

Braintree, Massachusetts.
Zanesville, Ohio.
Lemon Grove, California.
Sharon, Mississippi.
Granite City, Illinois.
Blytheville, Arkansas.
     Sweetwater, Texas.

## The Heart of the Hand

There is a language we say
when the lamp inside us
shows its face. Last night
playgrounds tilted
inside me, and music knocked
against the ends on my fingers.
I handed her a pool cue, fell
back and forth to the table
where she sat. I drove
down Westnedge with her
hand on my shoulder,
and the moment stood
up inside me for days.

A white line is chalked in
along the ground between us,
both of us in our bodies.
I have found a way across,
have taken this song by the hand
and brought it to this place.

## *Before the Reading, at a Philip's 66*

I am an imposter, writing to you
just this side of gasoline.

There are days I drive forty miles
for a human face.
I pull myself through people,
or fall away from my mouth.

Sometimes my heart knocks so hard,
waiting for the next word.

The trees will have to split
into pieces
to hold me.

# JOHN RYBICKI

## *After "The Star-Spangled Banner"*

Black lips pulse against the screen
as if there were an alien inside.
Then the television fizzes
to black and white dots.
My brother says it's the Russians
taking pictures of our brains,
drags on a joint until he's
squeaking like a duck. Maybe
the lights are just fists
pounding car hoods in traffic,
or the spots where black frogs
are leaping into another dimension.

## *Subterranean*

I

Every eye
on my skin pops
open. My ribs split
back and out
tears the heart,
a huge apple
dragging its threads.

I I

I take my medicine
canniballike,
my teeth in God's sides,
or breaking.

I I I

For decades
the old Chevy,
slapped with buckshot and driven
by country children,
slowly dives
into the woods out back.

I V

The rust on my tongue melts.
Then my house goes down
into the mud.

v

Greyhound, I chase
the wild rabbit,
knowing that white
thing on the pole
is really an angel.

## *That Miracle*

Your hands dial the stove,
navigate the morning. More
of fall sifting the patio screen,
the lady in the tub,
her brown hair beneath
the waterfall spout.

You travel at light speed
to this day, grateful
that when you extend your hand,
it does not go through her,
the ghost of some past love.
That miracle.

## *From the Room of the Body*

I sat on the downhill
of a street, tire-black
on my jeans, my hands
rubber-polished,
and could not move.
I am broken from trying,
from wrapping that other body
around the bolts on God's door,
as if man and woman together
could open it. Woman, new friend,
you are the fire
that washes off these words,
that almost cleans them.

## *Job*

I spray ammonia and water at a storm
window, buff it
with a rag, with pyjamas
puffed out at the belly.
I hold the window up
to catch smears.
A couple of leaves knock
against the driveway,
but I hear feet.
In this far yard,
it has been me all along.
Come home.

## Reading About Rita

How her father danced and
slept with her,
how her mother knew
but drank,
how Hollywood transformed her
into Hayworth,
how her husband offered her
to those who could help.
After that,
variations, variants, revisions.

## Helen and Ben

Saturdays
he took her shopping
for special cakes and herring.
They had no friends.
Their life filled up with apartments.
The vacancies. The tenants.
She cooked for him.
They watched television.

## That Day

That day my father would have run
into the streets, shouting my name,
if I had asked. He would have curled
up on his side under my bed—
if I had asked. He would have brought
my shoes tearfully to his lips,
praised my suspenders, embraced
my underwear in front of all
of the neighbors. If I had asked.

*Sliding Out at Home*

Beneath the mulberry, licking
the webbing of our thumbs, Jimmy
and I pretend
to know everything about girls:

the folds, the wrinkles, the on-and-
off switches. The ripened fruit we
crush on our palms
and snicker over. Pray over.

I hold two baseballs to my chest.
Jimmy takes them between his legs
and shouts, "Home plate!"
But the catcher has his mask off—

my father in his boxer shorts
coming out to start the mower.

## Lawrence

You first
likened my lips
to cracked earth. To cactus,
you remembered, all leaves are thorns.

## Poem

Then I lay like an oven
around it, fired clay. My
image. My lips to
its, my breath, something
I gave no animal.
By the time it woke
to its living, I had pulled
away. Watched
from the pines its sitting.
Standing. Its spread fingers
stroking. Not itself. Not
its powdery bed.
The air around it.
The emptiness. Not even
I foreknew that: that
clay remembers.

It takes
a quiet mind
to enjoy this

### IDEA FOR A MOVIE

A lonely writer in New York, thirty-ish male, spends all his time writing and never goes out.

The scene switches to L.A., to a woman—attractive, late twenties, an actress—shown by her pool with a cold drink and a couple of handsome young men gadding about.

Do you think this is a good idea for a movie, or should I think up another one?

### ANOTHER MOVIE IDEA

A punk drug abuser is shown holding up a 7-Eleven-type convenience store. The actual name of the store is disguised so we don't get sued. The camera shows a lot of the things for sale in the store—candy bars, milk, potato chips, cigarettes, magazines, etc.—but the brands are changed, disguised, so we wouldn't get into trouble with a lawsuit.

The scene switches to a police precinct with the usual detective banter. Some of the detectives are undercover, and it's only because they are in a police station that we realize they are police officers working undercover.

Do you think this is a good idea for a movie, or do you like the first one better? Both would be in color with music and talking and actual sounds. The first one would be a little longer, but they would both seem as long.

### ANOTHER IDEA FOR A MOVIE

The action takes place in outer space—a starship interior with stars seen moving by the window. The commander, motioning toward a control panel and looking out the window toward the stars, says to another officer, a navigator, "Bear left up here a ways—we should be in WACKSYS by 3 P.M."

The navigator asks, "To make the ship go left, do I turn

the wheel in the opposite direction like a boat, or in the same way like a car?"

The commander, immediately suspicious, knowing full well that the ship turns left by turning the wheel to the left like a boat, says, "Turn it left like a car."

The navigator says, "Okay, you're right like I thought."

The next scene takes place in a marina with a middle-aged gentleman driving up in a town car to the parking area. **Q**

So far
In the history of the world
Vincent van Gogh and Eric Clapton got the same birthday.
Flannery O'Connor and Lenny Bruce got the same deathday.
On the day Goethe died in 1832, Chico Marx was born
    in 1891.
Jack Kerouac was born on the day the Girl Scouts was formed.
Henrik Ibsen and Ozzie Nelson were born on the
    Vernal Equinox.
Nothing else happened on the day Uranus was discovered.
On the day Elvis died, Charles Bukowski celebrated
    his 57th birthday.
Twenty-three years after Tennessee Williams was born,
The Popeye statue was unveiled at the Spinach Festival
In Crystal City, Texas.
I would say things have worked out
Pretty well in the world.
So far.

THE DIFFERENCE BETWEEN MEN AND WOMEN

FIVE MODERN WOMEN JUST SOUTH OF TAOS

WHAT NEBRASKA WOULD LOOK LIKE WITH PYRAMIDS

RECENT FURNITURE THAT JUXTAPOSES
CLASSICAL AND MODERN FORMS

TOASTED REUBEN SANDWICH,
NAMED FOR REUBEN, SON OF LEAH
AND JACOB, THE SON OF ISAAC AND
REBECCA, FATHER OF ASHER,
BENJAMIN, DAN, GAD, ISSACHAR,
JOSEPH, JUDAH, LEVI, NAPHTALI,
SIMEON AND ZEBULUN

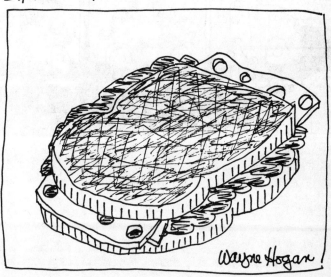

Wayne Hogan

GOOD NEWS/BAD NEWS

It is not enough that Béla Bartók, the last great Romantic composer, played baseball in Asheville, North Carolina. On the rooftops, grey-throated blackbirds twitter about; if you listen closely enough, they seem to be saying: "Dalhousie University, Dalhousie University." The night music section of the third movement of Concerto for Orchestra incorporates birdsongs Bartók heard while in the Carolinas. Does it matter what kind of birds? This is no treatise on the thrill of the grass; Bartók simply played second base for the Asheville Remission Tigers in their famous 1941 drive. The story is quite popular in Canada. Something about it expresses our simultaneous participation in and fear of American culture. It is not so incredible. Everywhere you look, unlikely people are getting the job done. Bartók batted right-handed, hit for average, good glove.

The third movement of the concerto is not as steady. When the middle infielder goes into his or her pivot, it is always the same; originality is never at stake—originality is a fig! You can tell that to your hero, Shostakovich. The ball leaves the fingertips and you know right away. Even a Blue Jays fan could tell you that. The doctors never tell you the whole story, and it's okay because the diagnosis is the same: goodbye. On the home field of the Asheville Remission Tigers, Béla Bartók looked to the future.

They were a feared nine. Uniforms of Napoleonic red with neon-yellow sabertooths clenching the words "Asheville Remission." In the batting circle, Bartók swung what today might be called the Kirby Puckett model—lightweight, quick to flip out. Paradoxically, he optioned for an open stance, a one-foot rising Sadaharu Oh-ish approach. Just about impossible to bust inside. It isn't always magic. But he doesn't get down on himself. The fans have a word for it: polycythemia. From the windows of the convalescent home: those stupid birds.

The Tigers' *Wunderjahr* shouldn't leave you cold. They worked hard to make it through the schedule and meet the Rocky Mount Palliative Bruins in the championship series. The Bruins had their fans, too, some who collected stamps, some who thought the Carolina outdoors were better understood drunk. But Bartók's genius for not sweating the competition, never disparaging a contemporary in public, gave the Asheville team a boost. Let them come on! He was not there to succumb to "listenability." A sonata for solo violin? With quarter tones? It's true, but don't forget to pitch and catch with your sons and daughters. Have a nap in the crowd. It isn't so serious. The smells of cigar smoke and beer spilled in the rampways are no longer in the stadiums. They now smell like malls, like fresh-pressed cotton shirts. And no matter where you turn, there are always unexplained momentos and snippets of brief (furious) psychological pain.

Bartók's wife, Ditta Pasztory, wasn't keen on the national pastime, but was glad to see Koussevitzky visit her husband in the sanitarium. She played the piano, waiting, and Bartók would rap out a final Texas Leaguer for her. It was a fundamental base hit. In 1941, Ted Williams of the Boston Red Sox hit .406—the last person to jack it over the *quadricentennial* mark. Bartók left Hungary to waste away in the music departments of American universities. Ethnomusicologically-speaking, he was a grunt. Use your noodle on the field, the body part should come naturally. "Ninety-nine percent of this sonata is half mental," Ditta remembered a piano coach saying.

It is not enough to say anything. There is no Act V pathos in the final match between the Remission Tigers and the Palliative Bruins. There were, however, quite a few hot dogs downed, and to this day people still talk about that game, even standing in the snow.

"In my youth," Bartók said, "I built up my legs by running up and down a mountain naked with my friends." The approved biography begins: "He was a sickly child." Awop-bopaloolapawopbamboo. You have to be strong but not stodgy-legged to survive the middle infield.

In conversation with Benny Goodman, Szigeti at the piano, Bartók, with a baton in his hand, asked the King of Swing who his favorite ballplayer was.

"It's you, Béla, it is you," Mr. Goodman said. **Q**

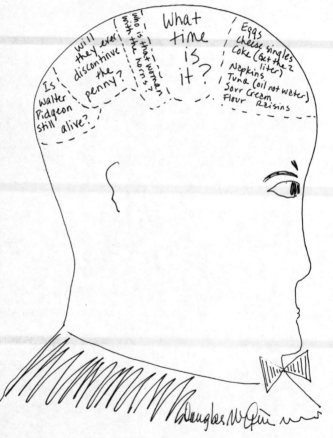

Doug's Thoughts On The New Production of Wagner's "Die Götterdämmerung"
(February 19 at the Metropolitan Opera in New York City, very near The GingerMan Restaurant.)

Is Walter Pidgeon still alive?

Will they ever discontinve the penny?

who is that woman with the horns?

What time is it?

Eggs
cheese singles
Coke (Get the 2 liter)
Napkins
Tuna (oil not water)
Sour Cream
Flour  Raisins

Douglas McGrath

Dear "Pres." of Recreation:

Well even if the Outing was canceled Sat. it was a Joy to have our "indoors Pic-Nic" in the Lounge + anyway outside we couldn't have the wild life program on J.V. could we? And I got to see my friends + Mr. Woolley even if we did have a "argument". Mr. Woolley is 92, he has trouble hearing, he thot I told Mr. Durham that he was nice, but I did not. Your Pic-Nic was lovely, you make us Old Senior Citizens feel like children which is so nice, you give us nice little surprises, even if you don't pay for them + anyway its your job + you get paid for it while we don't have anything anymore + have to live in this ~~sleasy~~ fucking shit-hole.

    Sincerely,
    (Mrs.) Enid Crackel

The Homestead—Hot Springs, Virginia. This is a huge, old, rambling place. A mountain resort, like Asheville. I have to admit it's a little boring here at the Homestead, but the old place is beautiful and they have an orchestra at five for tea. "The pace is quickening," said Mother when another couple (of whom most are aged) stopped for tea. I mean, this place has huge empty drawing rooms and game rooms and writing rooms and lobbies and endless public rooms, all beautifully appointed, with old camellia paintings and chintz armchairs and couches and potted palms and 25-foot ceilings with massive colonnades of white columns with Corinthian capitals and elaborate architraves and rugs. You look down endless halls of this magnitude with their huge columns and potted palms. The dining room is the same, with a vaulted ceiling and the endless columns and the hugeness. At dinner, there was an orchestra and dancing. Theo, aged two, gazed raptly at the orchestra. It was the kind of place where fathers danced with their little daughters on the dance floor. The children and their parents did a konga line. A little boy my nephew Al's age sauntered up. He was wearing a coat and tie. They make you get dressed up for dinner here. No one can walk around the hotel after seven without a coat and tie—formerly a tuxedo.

"What's your name?" I said to the little boy.

"George."

"Where are you from?"

He screwed up his face in a torture of thought, an agony of contemplation—thinking, trying, searching. Minutes passed. Naturally, I was going to tell him it was okay, he didn't have to know where he was from. But finally he came up with it.

"Rye."

"Rye, New York. Al's from New York, too," I said. "How old are you, George?" I asked.

"Five."

"Al's six."

They put their hands in their pockets and gazed at each other. It was love.

George pulled a key out of his pocket. "This is my room key," he said.

"This is *my* room key," said Al, and he procured a key from his pocket and displayed it proudly.

Then they raced off into the wild blue yonder.

The Homestead. Monday. The pace quickens whenever someone walks down one of the great halls, which is rarely. My vantage point is the game room. The place seems Northern. No hint of the tropics, or of our Gulf Coast environs. All genteel American, Old Virginia, sort of like the Adirondacks. No hint of the blazing tropic sun. The old spa is connected to the hotel and also has games such as Ping-Pong all inside, with a view to the mountains and the white painted wood of an old Northern spa. The invigorating air.

At dinner, George raced over in his little coat and tie. Mother noted that George has the manner of a Northern, not a Southern, boy. When you ask him a question, he clutches his head, he gesticulates wildly, he struggles, he searches for whatever it is he is trying to say or some knowledge such as the age of his sister—such a fact being wholly unknown to him. As Mother pointed out, he is sarcastic and dark and world-weary. He is world-weary at five. He has a raspy voice and seems very sophisticated, though not very knowledgeable, as above.

I asked him how old his brother is. He screwed up his face into the questioning glare which it is accustomed to mount when searching for knowledge. Searching for the answers.

"Five, six, seven, . . ." he posited, searching, wondering, then shrugged.

"He looks like he could be eleven or twelve," I said.

"Eleven, twelve, maybe ten, . . ." wondering, searching.

"Maybe he's nine or ten," I said.

Finally, the massive shrug of absolutely no knowledge whatsoever of the answer.

Same routine re his sister. "I don't know," he flatly allowed, after a little squinting into the distance, trying in vain to calculate her age.

"I hate my brother because he pushed me against the car door and I had to get stitches," he said. (This apparently happened on the drive from New York to the Homestead.)

It's so quaint when you ask him a question, because his knowledge is limited but his demeanor is sophisticated and world-weary in his little coat and tie. Mother said he is like something out of *Catcher in the Rye.* A little New York boy.

"What school do you go to?" we asked.

"Midland," he said with infinite world-weariness. "It's in Rye," he knew, after coming up with that yesterday.

He says he is leaving tomorrow, but I would not put his word as very reliable because he is very mixed-up. He says he is going to his grandmother's in Narragansett. He definitely knows his grandmother's is in Narragansett. I asked him what he was going to do there.

The massive, world-weary shrug. I think part of the quaintness is the energy he puts into the massive, world-weary shrug.

The big moment comes at five at tea in the Great Hall with an orchestra. Several people turn up. The black maid walks up and down the hall in her black uniform and white apron, a woman of ample proportions.

"The pace is quickening," said Mother with her sardonic wit as very little transpired and Father stifled a yawn.

We can't make out why his family seems rather frosty to us, and rather unenthused about George constantly racing off with Al. I would be happy if my child had friends, or made them so easily.

The first night at dinner, when George and Al raced off to the game room and were playing checkers, George's father came in and hissed at George that he'd better get back to the table or he wouldn't be allowed to meet Al at the pool the next morning. George and Al kept making secret assignations.

"What are you doing after lunch?" George would say with his surreptitious air to Al, making urgent plans.

"Seeing you," would say Al.

"Good. Let's meet at the pool."

Poor George would constantly come up to me and say, "Can Al come up to my room and play?" and I would say, "Yes, if your father says it's okay," and then his father, of course, would say no.

"We're not going to play checkers after dinner, so you'd better tell Al good-bye," he would say. Etc.

Noting George's little coat and tie, I said at dinner, "You have to get dressed up, huh."

"Yes, but I can make my tie go like this," he said, pulling one end of it until it choked itself into a strangled knot at his neck, disrupting his collar and face into a horrible contortion, pretending that he was having a fit, much to Theo's amusement.

George straggled along the great hall with his mother. "Mom, can I go to the store?" he said raspingly.

"Go to the store?" she said frostily.

"Can I go to the store to get something?"

"To get something?" in her high-toned New York way.

"I want to get some gum at the store."

"Gum?" she said as though it were an object of loathing.

We saw George's mother trying on a dress in the store and asking her husband, "Do you think this would be good for the White House?" And George reeling off the names of his father and brothers, a lot of whom had the middle name of Delano, so we speculated that maybe they are a political family or related to someone in office.

We can't tell whether they are really leaving today because George is so mixed-up.

Mark ran into George and Al the next morning in the hall. He made his usual greeting ("Give me some skin"), and both boys gave him the high five.

"Who *is* that?" said George to Al.

"It's Mark Clein," said Al in the tone he uses to signify that everybody ought to know who Mark Clein is, or, as Mark said, as if he were introducing Magic Johnson or Michael Jordan. "He's marrying my aunt," said Al.

Mother has a post on the front porch in a patch of sun where she watches the guests arrive. She says they drive up in their cars and take out clothes on hangers from the trunk instead of suitcases and then huge bottles of whisky. Gallon jugs of vodka.

Al said he wrote down George's room number on a piece of paper and then memorized it and went down and knocked on his door, Room 435. But no one answered. George, it appears, has indeed departed. **Q**

# PATTY'S BRAIN

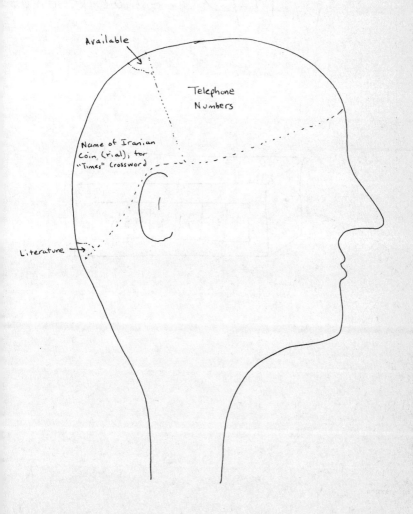

PATTY'S CLOCK

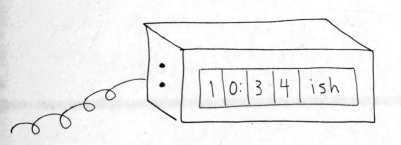

"Do you have tohalat today?" I say.

"Maybe tomorrow coming," the woman at the other end of the line says.

I put it out of my mind over the weekend. On Monday, I call again.

"Any tohalat today?" I say.

"Tohalat later coming," the woman says.

I push my way through the beaded curtain. The place smells like melon seeds. Cranky music comes from a radio somewhere in the interior. Up on the wall, on a plastic board, it says, "Tohalat, $2.50."

A woman comes out of the back room, wiping her hands on her apron. Her head is wrapped in a white scarf that hides her forehead.

"Do you have tohalat today?" I say.

"Today, no," the woman says. She flicks a crumb from the cash register.

"When will you have it?" I say.

"Maybe tomorrow," the woman says.

I say, "I come in for tohalat every time I'm in the neighborhood, and every time someone tells me maybe tomorrow."

The woman says, "This whole month if you came, we had tohalat. Today the boy who makes it is sick. The schwarma is good."

"Can I special-order the tohalat?" I say.

The woman shrugs. "Why special-order? We have every day," she says.

A man I've never seen is behind the counter when I go into the store the next day. I place my order.

"Tohalat finished," he says.

"You want to know what I think?" I say. "I don't think you ever have tohalat! I think you get people in here with the promise of tohalat and then you try to get them to buy the schwarma from you."

The man shrugs.

I say, "Could you please explain to me why tohalat is up there on the board but you never have any?"

The man looks at me and frowns. His expression is concerned, almost paternal. Then he nods. "You come back tomorrow between one and two. My wife make special for you," he says.


At 1:03 I go up to the counter. I say, "Tohalat, please."

The man turns. A smile flits across his lips.

"What tohalat?" he says.


The next morning, I put on a pair of lace-up shoes and a dark dress. Over it I wear a gabardine coat buttoned to the neck. I wrap my head in a white chiffon scarf. I take the end of the scarf and pull it over the lower half of my face before I go into the shop. I go up to the counter and order coffee. I sit at the front table and pretend to be reading. A notebook is hidden inside my paperback.

*11:50. A man with a moustache and a little girl in a pink dress come in. They go up to the counter. The woman behind the counter hands the man a small cylinder. The man hands it to the little girl. She tears it open and pops a Lifesaver into her mouth.*

*12:01. A man in work boots and a hard hat comes in. A few minutes later, the woman behind the counter hands him a pita sandwich. To go.*

*12:06. A group of people come in. They place their orders. I strain to hear. The woman behind the counter is putting something on a plate. Her back is to me. She turns, holding the plate. When she sees my face, her eyes narrow. The woman turns her back to me, covers the plate with foil and crimps the edges. Then she hands it to the man. She says something to him in their language. He grins a grin. A deal has been struck. Money changes hands. The only word I understand is tohalat.*

"Excuse me," I say to the man. "What is that on the plate?"

"No speak," he says.

*"Plate!"* I say. I point. "Tohalat?" I say.

He licks his lips. "Ah-h-h," he says. He nods and beams.

I let out my breath and suck it in again. In an even voice I say to the woman, "I'd like some tohalat."

"No tohalat. Only schwarma," she says. She waggles her finger at me.

The man nods and smiles. "Schwarma good," he says. He peels back the foil and holds the plate up for me to sniff.

I call at least thirty times during the week, around the clock. That there is no answer could mean the place is closed. This gives me limited satisfaction. I plan to be reasonable when the woman answers. I plan to say, "Have I, personally, done something to offend you? This whole unfortunate thing with Nablus and Gaza is not of my doing—."

One afternoon, the woman picks up in mid-ring. I cup my hand over the speaker. "Do you have tohalat?" I say in a hoarse croak.

At the other end of the line there is a long pause, a sudden intake of breath, a click, a dial tone. **Q**

HALLUCINATION ON 46ᵗʰ STREET

Dear Ms. Torron:

As to your letter concerning compensation and contractual arrangements for one's appearing in *The Quarterly*, I have consulted my attorney, and he advises me to make the following points:

As everyone knows, in 1987 *The Quarterly* published my fiction "Falling". My compensation was a year's supply of Cremora. At the time, it was sufficient, thrilling. I was unknown, working for the Transit Authority as a third-rail tester. However, the publication quickly won me acclaim. As a result, *The Red Hook Review* has offered to double any amount stipulated by you for my future work.

My attorney feels it is incumbent upon me to make you cognizant of this offer in order to forestall litigation should I be forced to break my relations with *The Quarterly* and/or your arm.

Your Most Gentle Servant,

John Lowry

P. S. Lest it escape your attention, bitch, I'm from Brooklyn.

Is it too true? If it is, it is too unreal. Lish Brothers—hats! Yes? Really? Tell me, no. Because years, years back there in my modeling years, I talked to them there at Lish Brothers. Not them, just her. I do not know who she was. I guess she was the runner of things. God knows her title. I certainly don't. I do not remember all of her, hardly even part of her. But only her mouth, I think. Tight and pinched, it was. No, not tight and pinched. It was full, but she made it pinched. She pinched it in. With little lines at the top of it going down into it. Into her mouth, I mean. Cat lines, I think you call them. Not the whisker lines that go across sometimes; I mean the lines that go up and down. Anyway, I seem to remember her mouth, her mouth more than anything else. How she kept pursing and pouting with it, sucking in and chewing on it with her teeth, tonguing it and licking it. At least, this is how I think I remember her, unless my mind is playing tricks on me and she wasn't mouth at all. But her lipstick was ruby red. I remember that. Ruby, ruby, it was ruby. I think, now that I think of it, that she was petite, small. With her ruby lips and with her red hair, too. Now it comes back to me—the hair. The color of her hair was something in the in-between of auburn and carrot. Please don't expect me to be exact on her color. One cannot expect one to be exact about a thing like that—color. Not after years on years. But I think she wore a page boy. No matter. It was her mouth that made her her. Talking and talking and talking, she never stopped talking. Put on a hat, she said. I did. Put on another and another. I did and did. A hat face, she said. You have a hat face. I guess you know, Gordon, you being the son and nephew of hatters, that a hat face can sell any hat. Those eyes under those brims, she said. What a look, she said. Those eyes, that face, she said. I looked at her from under the brims and never said a word. Not word one. Not one peep, not one squeak. I looked at her ruby mouth. Lish Brothers was my first go-see, you see. Gordon, do you know go-see? Go and see a man about a job. That's go-see. This was a woman. She stared at my hat face. Made me turn my hat face in all different directions. Look at the ceiling, she said. Look at the floor. Look into the corners of the room. Oh, Gordon, I remember, I remember, she pinched my chin and moved my head and made my eyes look into her eyes. A mouth, she said. You need a mouth. You've got to be able to talk hats, she said. The buyers, you've got to buy and sell the buyers, she said.

Was she your father's mistress, do you know?

No, no don't answer me. I should not have asked. It's just the way she ran things there. Like she owned things there. Most mistresses who also work for their lovers have a way about them, a way that says they own the place. They do own the place.

Gordon, please forgive me for asking such a terribly terrible thing about your father, of all people. God, how could I? Enough. I must not take up any more of your time. Only I had never made the connection of Lish and Lish. Lish the editor and Lish the hatters. All this time I know you, and my mind never goes from Lish to Lish. Christ, Gordon, is it true? **Q**

another message from God

FOR CREDIT-CARD ORDERS OF BACK NUMBERS, CALL TOLL-FREE,
AT 1-800-733-3000. PRICES AND ISBN CODES SHOWN BELOW.
OR PURCHASE BY CHECK OR MONEY ORDER VIA LETTER TO
SUBSCRIPTION OFFICE. NOTE ADDITION OF POSTAGE AND
HANDLING CHARGE AT $1.50 THE COPY PER EACH COPY REQUESTED.

| | | | | | |
|---|---|---|---|---|---|
| Q1 | $6.95 | 394-74697-x | Q11 | $7.95 | 679-72173-8 |
| Q2 | $5.95 | 394-74698-8 | Q12 | $7.95 | 679-72153-3 |
| Q3 | $5.95 | 394-75536-7 | Q13 | $8.95 | 679-72743-4 |
| Q4 | $5.95 | 394-75537-5 | Q14 | $8.95 | 679-72893-7 |
| Q5 | $6.95 | 394-75718-1 | Q15 | $9.95 | 679-73231-4 |
| Q6 | $6.95 | 394-75719-x | Q16 | $9.95 | 679-73244-6 |
| Q7 | $6.95 | 394-75936-2 | Q17 | $10.00 | 679-73494-5 |
| Q8 | $6.95 | 394-75937-0 | Q18 | $10.00 | 679-73495-3 |
| Q9 | $7.95 | 679-72139-8 | Q19 | $10.00 | 679-73690-5 |
| Q10 | $7.95 | 679-72172-x | Q20 | $10.00 | 679-73691-3 |